POPULAR CRAFTS
GUIDE TO
POTTERY

1987

POPULAR CRAFTS
GUIDE TO POTTERY

ALAN & GILL BRIDGEWATER

CHILTON BOOK COMPANY, RADNOR, PENNSYLVANIA

Argus Books Limited
1 Golden Square
London W1R 3AB

© Argus Books Ltd 1986

ISBN 0 8019 7722 3

Published in Radnor, Pennsylvania 19089, by Chilton Book Company.

British Library Cataloguing in Publication Data

Bridgewater, Alan
Popular crafts guide to pottery.
1. Pottery craft
I. Title   2. Bridgewater, Gill
738.1   TT920

ISBN 0-85242-860-X
ISBN 0-8019-7722-3 Chilton Ed.

Phototypesetting by En to En, Tunbridge Wells, United Kingdom
Printed and bound by R. J. Acford, Chichester, United Kingdom

CONTENTS

INTRODUCTION 1

Potters data. Clay types and preparation. Forming techniques. Moulding techniques. Casting and moulding using clay slips. The potter's wheel. Decoration. Glazes and glaze firing. Kilns, firing and loading

PROJECT ONE 25

MAKING JAPANESE RAKU TEA BOWLS

Introduction. Considering the project. Preparing the clay. Forming the thumb-pot base. Coiling the rim and foot. Decoration. Biscuit firing. Glazing and glaze firing. Hints, tips and notes.

PROJECT TWO 33

MAKING AN 'ARTS AND CRAFTS' OWL

Introduction. Considering the project. First steps. Making the basic body form. Shaping the owl body. Making the owl head. Modelling the form. Biscuit firing. Glazing. Glaze firing. Hints, tips and notes.

PROJECT THREE 43

MAKING A PERUVIAN SPOUTED CAT VASE

Introduction. Considering the project. First steps. Coiling up. Coiling and modelling the cat head. Coiling the spouted handle. Decoration. Burnishing. Firing. Hints, tips and notes.

PROJECT FOUR 55

MAKING AN AFRICAN TRIBAL POT

Introduction. Considering the project. First steps. Building and coiling the necked half-pot. Coiling up the base. Finishing, scraping and decoration. Firing and finishing. Hints, tips and notes.

PROJECT FIVE 65

MAKING AN ENGLISH MEDIEVAL INLAID TILE

Introduction. Considering the project. First steps. Making the plaster mould. Rolling and pressing the tile. Working the inlay. Biscuit firing. Glazing and firing. Hints, tips and notes.

PROJECT SIX   75

MAKING A CHINESE TRAY

Introduction. Considering the project. Preparing the clay and cutting the slabs. Cutting, fretting and piercing the tray sides. Piercing the clay. Putting together. Biscuit firing. Glazing and glaze firing. Hints, tips and notes.

PROJECT SEVEN   85

MAKING AN OLD ENGLISH TRAILED SLIPWARE DISH

Introduction. Considering the project. First steps. Press-moulding the dish. Preparing the slip and slip trailers. Decorating the dish. Trimming, fettling and biscuit firing. Glazing. Glaze firing. Hints, tips and notes.

PROJECT EIGHT   97

MAKING A NEW ENGLAND 'KEEPING ROOM' DISH

Introduction. Considering the project. Preparing and rolling the clay. Marbling the clay. Moulding the dish. Pulling the knob feet. The pie-crust edge and finishing. Drying, biscuit firing, glazing and glaze firing. Hints, tips and notes.

PROJECT NINE   107

MAKING AN ART DECO VASE

Introduction. Considering the project. First steps. Making the plaster mould. Slip casting the vase. Fettling or trimming the cast. Biscuit firing. Glazing. Glaze firing. Hints, tips and notes.

PROJECT TEN   117

MAKING A VICTORIAN DOLL'S HEAD

Introduction. Considering the project. Designing and making the working model. Making the plaster mould. Casting the doll's head with porcelain slip. Finishing and firing. Hints, tips and notes.

PROJECT ELEVEN   127

MAKING A COUNTRY COTTAGE JUG

Introduction. Considering the project. First steps. Working the clay. Opening up the clay. Forming the belly and neck of the jug. Pulling the lip. Pulling the handle. Slip decoration. Drying and biscuit firing. Glazing. Glaze firing. Hints, tips and notes.

A POTTER'S GLOSSARY   139

BIBLIOGRAPHY   145

INDEX   148

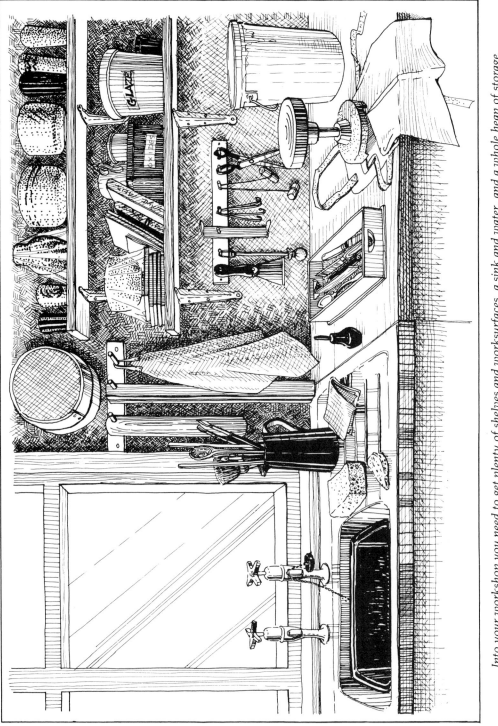

Into your workshop you need to get plenty of shelves and worksurfaces, a sink and water, and a whole heap of storage cupboards and boxes. Brushes, sieves, plastic containers, pencils, rolling pins and slip trailers; they can all be obtained from a specialist supplier.

INTRODUCTION

Pottery making is a uniquely exciting craft — to drink out of a bowl or cup that you have shaped and seen through the rigours of firing — to take a piece of pottery from the kiln and to know that but for you, it would still be a shapeless lump of wet clay . . . these are all wonderfully exciting experiences.

The aim of this book is to introduce the beginner to what has come to be called, 'craft' or 'studio' pottery, and to lead him through the craft with a series of progressive projects. We go through the various techniques and we do our utmost to blow away all the mystique and reveal pottery making for what it is, an absorbing craft, a craft that can be worked in the home, an exciting leisure activity and a fascinating adventure. In our Potters Data we briefly describe the workshop and all the making stages from forming to firing, then we go straight into the craft with eleven structured and detailed step-by-step projects. Each project has a short introduction that relates it to a particular folk or ethnic tradition, then we follow this up with dozens of 'hand-on-tool' illustrations. Each project deals in depth with a particular pottery technique and form, and covers everything from the initial design concepts through to taking the pot from the kiln.

We don't meander — with our 150 or so illustrations we get right down to the foundations of the craft, and tell you in no nonsense terms, why, when, how and what with. Of course pottery making is unpredictable, but here-in lies the challenge. Work through our projects — make an African pot, an Art Deco Vase, a Country Jug or whatever, and not only will you beautify your home, but you will be able to tell all your friends . . . "I made it!" . . . what a feeling!

POTTERS DATA

FROM THE WORKSHOP TO THE KILN

The Workshop   If you have started going to pottery classes, joined a

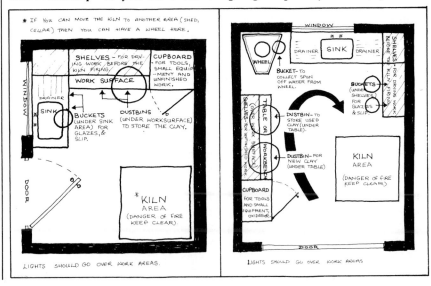

LEFT *Your workshop can be set up in quite a small area — draw up a groundplan with special reference to windows, doors, water, worksurfaces and power.*

RIGHT *If you are going to specialize on say the wheel, then you need to shape your workshop layout accordingly. See how there is a nice flow from the clay bins to the kiln.*

There are any number of possible layouts — if it's got a window, a door, water and power, then it's got workshop potential.

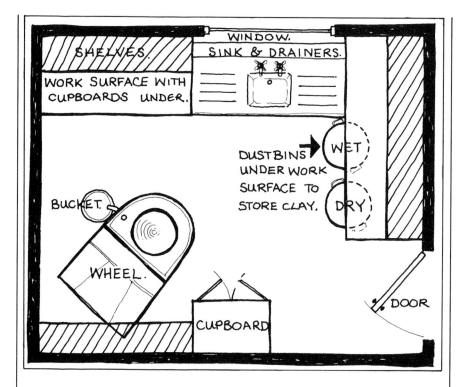

ceramics group, or are a self-taught beginner, sooner or later you will feel the need to set up your own home workshop or studio. This workshop need not be a grandiose affair with massive wood fired kilns and huge pieces of equipment — we have had students setting up workshops in everything from a cellar to an old chicken shed at the end of the garden. If it has got a floor, a roof, four walls, a window, a door, power and water — then it's got workshop potential.

Let's say then that you are considering turning the spare room into a workshop and that you have a floor area of about one hundred square feet — say a room 10×10 feet. Into this relatively small space you need to get plenty of shelves and worksurfaces; a sink and water, a small kiln, maybe a potters wheel, and a whole heap of storage cupboards and boxes. Of course, after the initial run-through of the various techniques, you will want, as likely as not, to concentrate on one technique, say throwing, slabbed, coiled or whatever; so in the first instance we will talk you through the pottery making processes and stages, and then you can re-shape the advice and suggestions to suit your own individual needs.

Clay   Red and white earthenware, stoneware, Raku and porcelain clays all arrive from the supplier in easy to handle ½ cwt plastic bags — so where to put them? If you're only buying a couple of bags, then no problem, but if you want to cut down your costs and buy say half a ton at a time, then you need a clay store. Ideally clay must be stored in cool, frost-free conditions — in the garage, under your worksurfaces or in an outside bunker. If clay is kept cool and damp, then it will keep indefinitely. Also of course you don't want to be hauling ½ cwt bags up and down stairs, or from the end of the garden, so think on it! We keep clay stock in the garage and then bring a bag into the workshop as and when it is needed.

The Claybench Clay needs to be prepared — that is, wedged, banged and kneaded before it can be used, so you must have a good stout workbench. Ideally you need a bench or table that has a scrubbed solid wood surface, and four, strong, well braced legs.

Don't bother with a plastic covered table because the laminate will only crack and curl — go for, that is make or buy, a table that has a plain unsealed wood surface. To test a bench, take up as much clay as you can reasonably lift, hold it chest high, then bang it down — if the table sits four-square and doesn't complain, then it's fine, but if it bounces round the workshop, then you need to think again.

Storage and Shelves Your workshop must have as much storage space as possible — racks, shelves, old tea chests and cupboards, these can all be used. Aim to set-out and plan the workshop so that there is a good flow of shelves, cupboards and worksurfaces from the making bench through to the glazing area and kiln.

Clay Bins When you have made a pot — coiled, slabbed or whatever, you will have clay waste, everything from almost dry chips to handfuls of wet slop. Get yourself three lidded dustbins — one for water, slops and breaking down — one for clay that is drying out prior to being dropped in the breaking down bin, and one for clay that is still plastic and workable.

Glaze Storage Glaze powder arrives in plastic bags — it all looks the same no matter what type of glaze, that is a pinky, grey or white powder. As the glaze arrives, store it in well lidded and labelled containers, and as soon as you mix a batch of glaze, transfer it to a lidded and labelled bucket.

Sinks and water Pottery is a wet process — wiping down worksurfaces, washing out jugs, bowls and pots, mixing slips and glazes, and so on. You do need running water, a sink, a draining board, and plenty of old towels and cloths.

General storage Oxides, tools, kiln furniture, books, catalogues and bits of small equipment all need to be popped in drawers, boxes, or cupboards —you do need as much storage space as possible. Try and be organized and most important of all, label everything.

A space for the kiln If you are a beginner to pottery and you only have a limited workshop area, then you can't do better than to get yourself a modern electric kiln. OK, small electric kilns do have their limitations, but this is off-set by their cost, controllability and efficiency. If you want to fit a kiln into your workshop space, rather than say in another area, our advice is to visit a supplier's showroom armed with groundplans, a tape measure, details of your power supply, and see what they have to offer.

The potter's wheel and where to put it   There are geared kick-wheels, electric wheels, DIY wheels, some with seats and some without, and so on (see section on wheels), so how big and where to put it? The wheel needs to be near the workbench and sink, and if it's electric, then near to a power supply. So once again, measure up your workshop area, decide just how you prefer throwing, that is sitting or standing, then visit a showroom and see what's on offer. Note, if you look through the projects you will see that only one of them uses a wheel, so if you are short of space and anyway prefer making slabbed pots or whatever, then maybe a wheel does figure in your workshop layout.

Your tools — you need (a) Whirler turntable, (b) Batts and plastic containers (c) Jug and brushes (d) Glaze or clay bucket (e) rolling pin and cloth (f) Guide sticks (g) slip trailer (h) needle pricker (i) cutting wire (j) natural sponge (k) ruler (l) rubber kidney (m) metal kidney (n) scraper (o) clay knife (p) turning tool (q) burnishing spoons (r) large sponge.

Workshop tools and small equipment   Now you have a workshop with plenty of shelves and storage, a workbench, wheel etc — all you now need are a few tools and bits of table equipment. A banding wheel so that you can slowly turn your work round, measuring and thickness sticks, battens, a rolling pin, workboards or batts, rubber kidney tools, needle prickers, (see glossary), these can all be obtained from a specialist supplier, made or 'found'. For example you can't better a piece of sacking for rolling out clay, goose feathers for slip trailing, an old hair brush for clay beating, and so on. If you can't afford to buy tools, then make your own. Potters tend to be make-do-and-mend individualists; a bit of wet washleather for clay smoothing, an old plastic comb for textures, a needle pushed in a cork for a pricker — if it works for you, then it's a valid tool.

CLAY TYPES AND PREPARATION

Potters need clay — a good steady supply of workable, plastic, reliable clay. Yes you can search around for a local pit and then go and dig your own, and it's certainly good fun as a one-off mid summer experience, but you can take it from us, clay digging is backbreaking and anyway, who wants to be a clay digger? No, our advice is to make contact with a supplier and get him to send you prepared plastic clay, then you can spend those warm summer days making pots and not breaking backs.

The following clay list will give you some idea of clay types, their uses and characteristics.

Red earthenware   A good clay for beginners — red/brown in colour — it can be smooth, sandy or grogged and it fires to a temperature of around 1000–1100°C. A clay of this character is suitable for slipware, throwing, coiling, handbuilding and sculpture, and better still, it's reliable, relatively inexpensive and very pleasant to use. Traditionally most 'peasant' or 'folk' wares were made from red earthenware.

White earthenware   A smooth sandy or grogged grey/white clay that fires to a temperature of around 1100°C. A clay of this character is suitable for throwing, coiling and handbuilding. It biscuit fires to a creamy colour and looks good with slips or under clear and 'art' glazes. If you want to make slip decorated wares, then you need to use white or red earthenware clay, and both red and white slips.

Stoneware clay   Stoneware clays tend to be grey/blue/white in colour, and when fired to a temperature of around 1250–1300°C they become gritty with

Your clay might be described as 'prepared', but it will still be rough and full of air pockets — your clay needs to be wedged and kneaded.

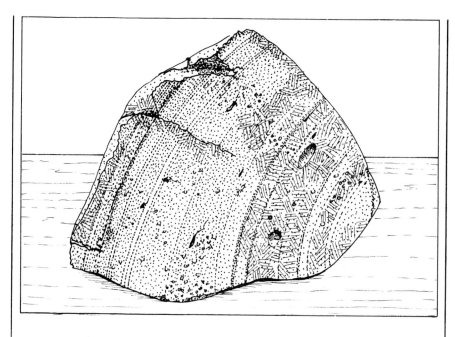

a stone-speckled texture. Some named stoneware bodies have added ingredients, for example a stoneware body might have a small percentage of red clay that fires out to a pinky brown, or a small amount of red iron oxide that fires out to give a rusty colour. A clay of this character is suitable for large thrown ovenwares, coiled and slabbed sculptures and most modern 'art' wares. It is usually fired under ash or 'Leach' type glazes.

Raku   A coarse clay with a high proportion of added grog, (fired and ground clay). Raku resists sudden 'in-and-out' kiln temperature changes, fires at 750–1000°C to a white or buff colour and can be used for large sculptural forms or small Japanese type wares.

Porcelain clay   Porcelain bodies are made up from china clays, feldspar, ball clays, etc. They fire to a high temperature of between 1150–1300°C, and become hard, vitreous and glassy. Porcelain clays can be used for fine domestic wares, delicate 'art' sculptures and of course dolls heads, (see project).

There are many other named clay types and bodies that are difficult to label, for example semi-porcellaneous china and bone china type clays. Our advice is to look through a supplier's catalogue, order sample packs, and use them and see how they fit into your scheme of things.

Clay preparation   When plastic clay comes from the supplier it arrives in ½ cwt bags and although it is described as being 'prepared', it still needs to be further wedged and kneaded to make sure that it is consistent in colour and texture, and completely free from air pockets, hard lumps and unknown bits of this and that.

Wedging If air pockets become trapped in clay when the pot is being fired, it will almost certainly shatter and spoil neighbouring pots and maybe even shelves and elements. So even though 'prepared' clay looks to be workable, always wedge and knead it just to be on the safe side.

For wedging you need a stout clay bench, ideally one that has a plain plank-wood, concrete or unglazed tile surface. Cut off a large manageable lump of clay, say about the size of a large loaf, bang it down on the table, and

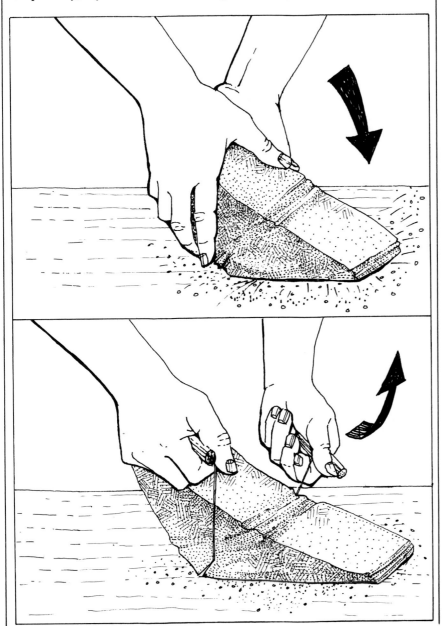

Take up as much clay as you can manage, and wham it down on the worksurface (wedging).

Wedging – Take your wire, slide it under the clay and then up – your clay should now be neatly halved.

Wedging – Finally, take one half of the clay and smash it down on its partner – notice how the pockets of air pop and bang.

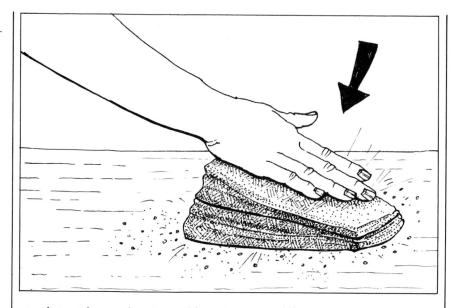

smack it with open hands until it is sharp ended. Now take the loaf shaped lump in both hands, and with considerable force, wham it down on the bench so that the end nearest you is slightly raised up. This done, take a cutting wire, and in a single movement, slide it away from you halfway under the raised end of clay, and then up! Your long loaf of clay should now be neatly halved.

Now take the half nearest you, turn it round so that you can see the cut face, then, holding it in 'praying' palms, send it crashing down onto the clay on the workbench. Finally, with open hands, beat the clay back into the original loaf shape. And so you continue, that is repeating the wedging work-out about ten to twenty times until you are sure that the clay is free from air pockets. Wedging is of course hard work, but you will soon learn to swing your arms with an easy rhythm, and your efforts will pay-off with fewer kiln breakages.

Kneading – take a lump of wedged clay and knead it with a rolling, 'push-and-pull', action.

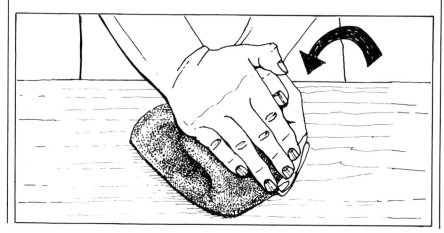

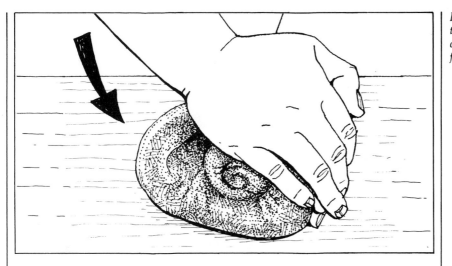

Kneading – work the clay until it looks to be tightly shell-coiled and smooth, consistent in texture, and totally free from lumps, bits and air pockets.

Kneading When you are ready to use your clay, that is after it has been wedged and maybe stored, it has to be brought to a good workable state with a few minutes kneading. Place a manageable lump of wedged plastic clay on the work surface, and in an easy shoulders-and-arms pushing and pulling action, push the clay down and away. Continue to work the clay, pushing and rolling, pushing and rolling, until it looks to be tightly coiled and shell-like, then it will be in prime working condition.

Re-cycling the clay; Wet clay Sooner or later, when you have been working on the wheel or making slip decorated dishes, you will have a bucket or so of wet clay and slop — this needs to be spread out on a board or plaster slab, air dried and then wedged and kneaded, as already described.

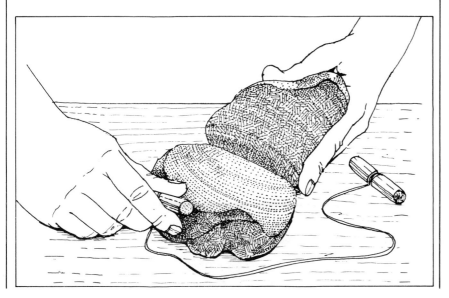

Kneading – when you have worked the clay, cut it in half with a wire and check it out for air pockets and bits of hard clay.

Recycling — you need at least two dustbins and either a workboard or plaster slab — see how the clay is dried, put into the wet bin and the resultant slop air dried.

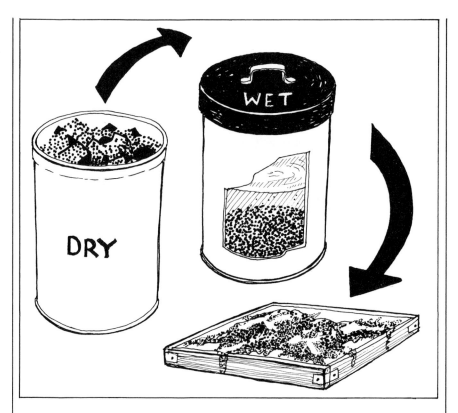

Dry clay   If you have any hard clay waste, that is to say pots that have broken before they can be biscuit fired, or scraps of clay that are dry and 'chalky', just break them into small pieces and drop them in water. After twenty-four hours or so, take the resultant wet slop, and work it as already described.

Leather-hard clay   Never put leather-hard scraps of clay into the 'wet' bin because they will resist water and stay leathery indefinitely. Let it dry off until it is 'chalky', then take it through the wet bin stage before wedging and kneading. Note, when you have recycled clay it tends to become 'weary', so let it sit a while in the clay store before using.

A pug mill   If you are really keen, and find yourself using large amounts of clay, then get yourself a small pug mill. These 'sausage' machines have a feeding hatch at one end, and a long spout mouth at the other. The idea is simple enough — you bung in a mixture of sloppy to firm clay waste, pull down a lever, and out of the spout comes a long sausage of workable, ready to be wedged and kneaded clay — a great labour saver.

   Two final points — if new or recycled clay is to stay workable, then it must be covered with a plastic sheet or stored in a damp cupboard and clay can be used and reused as long as it hasn't been fired above a black/red heat. If clay breaks down in water, then it can be recycled.

FORMING TECHNIQUES

PINCHING, COILING AND SLABBING

Making a basic pinched thumb pot   Take an apple sized lump of wedged and kneaded clay and smack it into a ball. Now hold the ball in one hand, thrust the thumb of the other hand into its centre, and then with a rhythmic pinching action of thumb and fingers, pivot the clay on your thumb. As the clay is turned and pinched, so it will grow in size and shape.

A small pinched thumb-pot of this character can either be used as the foundation for a much larger form, say the base of a huge coiled pot, or it can be a bowl or dish in its own right. If you want the pinched pot to become functional, say a little soup bowl, then it needs a foot or base ring. Roll out a little worm of clay, make a small ring, place the ring on the base of the upturned pot, and finally, with thumb and fingers, work the two together.

Making a basic coiled form   Take a manageable lump of prepared clay, and with flat hands and outstretched fingers, roll it out on the workbench. Aim to make 'worms', 'snakes' or coils of clay that are even and smooth along their length, and free from lumps, bumps and cracks. It is most important that the clay remains soft and workable, so as you make the coils, put them under a damp cloth or plastic sheet. If you are going to make a coiled pot, you will need a foundation or base on which to build — you can either work up from a little pinched thumb-pot, as already described, or you can coil up from a squashed ball 'pill'. Either way, once you have established a firm base, you add coils and work them together with thumb and fingers. As coils are added and worked one on top of another, so you have to control and shape the growing pot with a continuous 'hand-and-tool' action of turning, smoothing and beating. And so you work, adding coil upon coil. If you want the growing cylinder of clay to swell out, then you add the coils to the outside

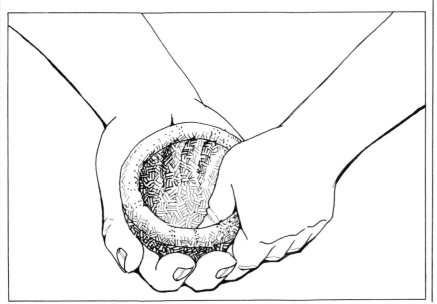

Pinched Thumb-pot — thrust your thumb into the centre of the ball of clay and then rotate the clay with a pinching action of thumb and fingers.

Coiling – coil up from a firm base, add coil upon coil and work them together with thumb and fingers – as the pot grows, so you will have to control its shape with a continuous smoothing, turning and beating action.

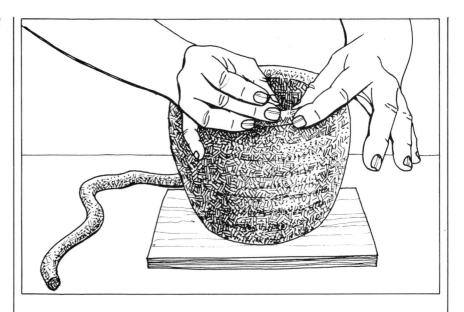

rim and if you want the form to narrow, then you add the coils to the inside rim. Bear in mind that coiling is a free 'keep the pot moving' process of adding, squeezing, shaping and gently persuading.

Making a basic slab-built form   Ceramic geometry slabbing is a 'box-building' method of making straight sided angular forms with sheets of clay.

Slab Built – allow the slabs of clay to stiffen, then with knife, metal straight edge and slip, build boxed forms.

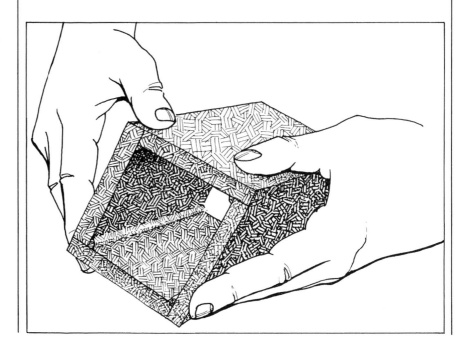

Spread a piece of sacking, or coarse cloth, on the worksurface and then with a rolling pin (like pastry making), roll out slabs of clay that are an even thickness of about ¼–½ inch. Now allow the slabs to stiffen so that they can be stood on edge without buckling. Then with a knife, measure, a metal straight edge, coils and slip, simply build boxed forms (see Chinese Tray project).

MOULDING TECHNIQUES

PRESS OR SLAB MOULDS

Making a press moulded form Have your slightly dampened mould to hand, that is to say a plaster of paris 'dip' or 'hump' mould, then with a rolling pin, rolling out cloth, two guide sticks, etc. roll out a ¼–½ inch thick slab of clay. This done, take up the clay-on-cloth, and lay it cloth uppermost in or over the mould. Now with a damp sponge and a rubber kidney tool, ease the clay so that it follows the mould profile. Now gently peel away the cloth and continue working the clay until it's smooth and free from wrinkles, bumps, cracks and air pockets. Finally, with a knife or cutting wire, trim away the surplus rind of clay from the edge of the moulded slab, then smooth the cut edge with damp fingers, a sponge or a piece of washleather. As the clay gradually dries and shrinks away from the plaster, so it will stiffen up. When it is firm enough to take its own weight, then it can be removed from the mould.

As regards form, shape and methods of decoration, both 'dip' and 'hump' moulded dishes can have coiled additions: feet, base rings, knobs, handles and the like and they can also be decorated with slips and oxides — see projects. There are in fact endless variations on the slab moulding theme — you can make oven crocks with moulded bottoms and lids, and slab built sides — you can coil up from slab moulded bases or you can build sculptural forms by joining moulded shapes rim to rim, base to base, or whatever.

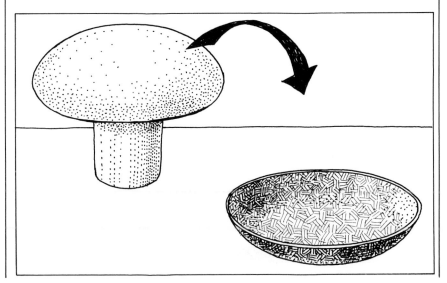

Press Mould — ease the rolled out slab of clay over the mould, let the clay dry out, then, when the clay is firm enough to take its own weight, lift it clear of the mould.

Although moulds are best made from plaster, wood or even biscuit fired clay, it is possible to also use 'found' forms. So for example you might mould clay in, or over, say a dustbin lid or plastic bucket — you simply dust the form with clay powder, ash or sand, just prior to moulding, and then work as already described. Bear in mind however, that as clay dries so it shrinks. It wouldn't work if you wanted to mould clay completely over a ball or over a sharply angled form — there must be plenty of room for clay shrinkage.

CASTING AND MOULDING USING CLAY SLIPS

Slip casting can be tricky, so if you are a complete beginner, don't get involved in making your own slips and moulds — it's a complicated business, but rather buy in ready-made slips and moulds.

Casting slips, equipment and tools   You need a basic casting slip which you can buy as dry separate ingredients, say ball clay, china clay, soda ash and so on, or you can buy a ready 'just add water' mix. As for tools and equipment, you need a simple two-piece plaster mould and such items as: a sponge, plastic jugs and containers, a timer, a whirler turn-table, a knife and glazing sticks.

Pouring the slip   Have the dusted damp plaster mould at the ready, then take the mixed, stirred lump-free slip and fill up the mould so that the slip starts to overflow. Now watch carefully, and when the slip level starts to drop, keep the mould topped up. From time to time, tilt the mould slightly so that you can see the thickness of the slip build-up on the mould walls, and

Slip Casting — when the slip build-up within the mould is dry and firm, carefully ease the two halves of the mould apart and remove the cast.

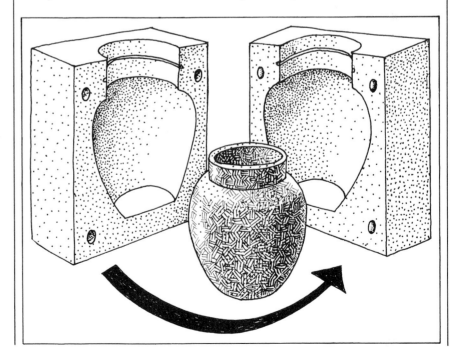

when the build-up is about twice as thick as that required (this will depend upon the size of the pot to be cast), pour off the surplus slip and leave the mould upside down to drain and dry.

With slip casting there are so many variables that it's very difficult to lay down specific hard and fast rules — room temperatures, the amount of water in slips, the type of mould, and so on, they are all critical factors. It's a good idea to experiment with one particular mould and slip, and to always keep notes of times, drying conditions and the like, then you will be able to work out your own rules of thumb, and also predict just how such and such a mould works. We usually leave the slip in the mould for about twelve minutes before pouring off and draining and after 1½–3 hours, when the cast starts to come away, open the mould. When you are ready to open the mould, always ease the two halves (could be several pieces) apart and if all is correct, the cast can be turned out.

Finally, when the cast pot is dry enough to handle, then fettle and trim the edge seams and casting waste. If you want to put together various castings, say handles to jugs, or spouts to teapots, then dab the joints with slip and very gently ease and work the clay until the joint is nicely welded and smooth.

THE POTTER'S WHEEL

TYPES, CHARACTERISTICS AND USING

Most beginners want, usually sooner than later, to have a go on a potter's wheel — a lump of prepared clay on a spinning wheel-head and the creative heave as the clay grows up and out is a uniquely satisfying experience. So what are the main characteristics of a good wheel? There are small stand-up models with iron wheels and cranks, there are some powered by electricity and some foot operated and so on. If you are a beginner, go for a wheel that has an infinite number of variable speeds, an adjustable well padded seat, a large easy to clean slop tray, a selection of removable wheel-heads, plenty of power, and make sure your chosen wheel is of a shape and size to resist vibrations and shudders.

As for tools and extras, you need a plastic bucket to catch the water and clay slip, a couple of side bowls for water, a hand-held sponge and a sponge on a stick, a cutting wire or cord, a ruler and calipers, a selection of wood or fibre batts, a needle pricker and a couple of turning tools.

Throwing — the basics Throwing a pot isn't any more difficult than say riding a bicycle or learning to swim — students can pick up the basics in a couple of hours. However throwing is a technique that does require a deal of concentration and hand, eye and mind co-ordination so you need to be keen. There are one or two points to clear out of the way before we start — you don't have to be especially strong, nor do you need to be stripped to the waist and swamped with water; much better in fact to use as little water as possible and to wear an absorbent cotton cover-all smock. Finally, for safety's sake, avoid dangling hair, drooping ties, bulky dress rings and wrist watches.

The basic throwing technique Wipe the wheelhead with a damp sponge and then, with a steady hand and a straight eye, smack an apple sized ball of

Go for a wheel that has an infinite number of variable speeds, an adjustable seat, a large easy to clean slop tray, a selection of removable wheelheads, plenty of power, and make sure that your wheel sits firm and square without judders and shudders. Notice the counterbalance foot control, the foot rest, and the back shelf.

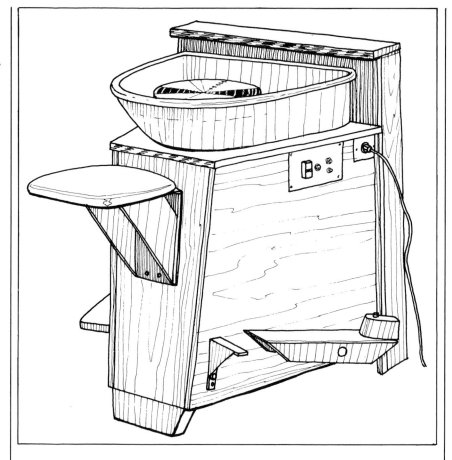

clay onto the centre of the motionless or spinning wheelhead. Now moisten both hands, and then, with both arms well braced and tucked into your waist, push the clay across the wheel with the left hand and down with your right. When you can cup the mound of spinning clay without it juddering or wobbling, it is centred. This done, dampen your hands again, place your braced and cupped hands over the spinning clay, and then with an easy in-and-up movement, pull the clay up into a cone shape. Now cup the cone of clay, and with a firm action, press down and re-make the mound. Aim to 'cone up' and 'mound down' until the clay feels well worked — say five or six times.

Opening the clay Push down on the spinning, well worked, clay with either your thumb, thumbs or a couple of fingers, until you reckon that there is about ½–¾ inch of clay between your finger tips and the wheelhead. Now brace your wrists and touch thumbs and with a gentle 'up-and-out' action, draw up the sides of the clay mound. When you feel that the fat cylinder of clay is about the right height, very carefully take your hands away, making sure that you don't whip your fingers off and drag the clay off centre.

Thinning the clay is straightforward — with either linked thumbs, or touching thumb knuckles, and the fingers of the left hand inside the pot, slowly draw the walls of the cylinder up. Try and achieve a cylinder of clay that is stable and has walls of an even thickness. Note — if you are working on a really large pot, you might have to use the clay with clenched fists and knuckles, rather than delicate finger tips.

The form and the rim   Have down on paper, or in your mind's eye, a clear picture of how you want your pot to be, then, with the fingers of the right hand on the outside, start to carefully draw out the form. Now, with thumb-tips touching, index fingers bent and crooked, and middle fingers touching, apply slight pressure round the pot neck and gently stroke your linked hands up-and-off. Finally take up the potters needle or pricker tool, trim off the ragged edge from the spinning pot, and then with a sponge or fingers, collar and smooth the cut edge until it is pleasantly round in section.

Taking the pot from the wheel   When you feel that the thrown form is finished, take the sponge on a stick, and with the pot still slowly spinning, mop out all the loose water. Now take a turning tool and bevel and clean up the foot of the pot. This done, splash a little wheel-slip on the wheelhead and with a taut thumb pressed wire, slice the pot off. Now this is where most beginners lose their nerve and let the pot slip from their grasp — so be warned! Have a batt or carrying tile dampened and at the ready, wipe your hands dry, then either cup the pot in both hands and lift it onto a batt, or palm-push the pot across the water puddled wheelhead onto a batt — either way, take care.

Throwing might appear initially to be almost impossibly finger twisting, but believe you me it's a knack — the secret is total concentration, and then practice and more practice.

DECORATION

A GLOSSARY OF BASICS

Burnishing   While the clay is leather hard, the surface is rubbed and compacted with a smooth tool, say the back of a spoon or a flat bone. Burnishing is usually worked with red earthenware clay and oxide slips — see project.

Impressed decoration   While the clay is still soft and workable, marks are made with stamps, fingers and various push-poke tools — impressed marks catch glaze and create pools of colour. This method of decoration can be used with all manner of wares and glazes.

Incised line   At the green or leather-hard stage the clay can be cut and gouged with a variety of knives and comb-like tools. An incised line can be restrained and organised, that is to say patterns and motifs, or it can be an overall scratched texture.

Inlay   At the green or leather-hard stage the clay is cut and worked. The cut hollows, or pools, are filled with clay or slip of another colour, and finally, when the clay is hard but still workable, the surface is carefully shaved to

Incised line — at the green or leather-hard stage cut and work the surface of the clay. The incised lines can be restrained and organized or as an overall texture.

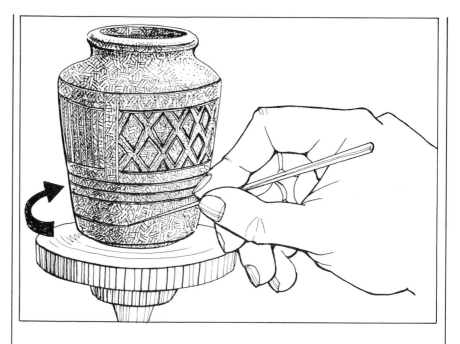

reveal a pattern that is characteristically clean and hard edged. This is a good technique for flat bold graphic pattern (see project on tiles).

Majolica   Majolica pigments are painted onto the powdered glaze surface at the pre-glaze firing, and the pot is covered with another thin glaze and then fired. There are of course any number of majolica methods that involve

Slip Painting — slips, and oxide coloured slips, can be brushed onto soft or leather-hard clay — see how the turning action of the banding wheel and the long haired brush aids and encourages free flowing designs.

stencils, transfers, sprays, glaze textures and so on — use these when you have grasped the basics (refer to suppliers catalogue).

Slip painting   Clay slips and oxide coloured slips are brushed onto the surface of soft or leather-hard clay to achieve a painted design. The characteristic designs are worked with long soft-haired brushes and generous amounts of thick, creamy, lump-free slip. Painted slip designs can be burnished or glazed with a clear or 'honey' glaze.

Slip trailing   This technique is best managed on broad flat surfaces, say dishes, slabs, tiles and the like. When the clay is still soft, it is given a slip coating or ground, then the design is worked with thick 'squeezed out' coloured slips. There are any number of traditional folk and ethnic slip techniques. Slips can be combed, feathered, marbled and trailed to form characteristic patterns, designs and motifs.

Sgraffito   Meaning to scratch. The damp clay is given a coloured slip coating, say red slip over a white base, and when the slip is dry the cover-coat is scratched to reveal the colour beneath.

Underglaze   At various stages, coloured pigments are brush applied, for example pigments that are painted on to pots at both the pre-biscuit and the pre-glaze stage might be called underglaze.

Wax resist   Hot wax is painted onto the surface of a green or biscuit pot so that it resists coatings of slip, oxide, glaze or whatever — wax resist burns out to leave characteristic 'roll-edge' marks and patterns.

GLAZES AND GLAZE FIRING

Basically a glaze is a glassy coating which is used to make a pot water-tight and decorative. There are a great many traditional glaze types: alkaline, boracic, lead, tin, ash etc, and although you can buy them as basic dry ingredients, we would always advise beginners to go for 'just add water' pre-mixes.

Glaze preparation   Clear your worksurface and have at hand the bag of glaze powder, a set of scales, a sieve or lawn, a sieve mop, water, a plastic bucket, various plastic bowls and containers and a sponge. Carefully weigh out the glaze powder, as described by the supplier, for the amount required, say one gallon or two, then put it in a bucket and add water. This done, stir the mixture until it is thick and creamy, then with the sieve and sieve mop, pass it into another bucket. Finally, when the glaze has passed through the sieve and is free from lumps and bits and pieces, label both the bucket and the lid with a permanent marker.

Putting on the glaze, pouring and dipping   If your pot is large, then pouring is probably the best method. Swiftly glaze the inside of the pot, that is to say fill it with glaze and then empty and drain, then place the pot upside down on battens over a bowl, and be ready with a jug of glaze. Now take the

Sieve the glaze with a lawn and glaze mop — make sure that it is creamy and free from lumps and bits. Pass the glaze through the sieve and into a labelled and lidded container.

To glaze the inside of a pot, simply fill it up with liquid glaze, then empty and drain.

Dipping — hold the pot by its foot and swiftly slide it in and out of the well stirred glaze.

jug, and slowly walk round the pot pouring as you go. Try for an even coverage and a nice steady flow. Finally, when the glaze is dry, get a damp sponge and clean off the pot base.

Dipping   Add water to, or take water from the glaze mix, as the case may be, give it a good stirring, then finger grip the pot by its foot and in a swift considered movement, slide the pot in and out of the glaze, Now wait a moment for the glaze to dry, and then wipe off the pot base. The glaze should cover the pot with an even 'chalky' coating — there must be no re-dippings, brushings or fussing about, If you don't like your efforts, wash the glaze off, let the pot dry, and then try again. Note — pots in the 'just been glazed' state look matt white, cream or grey; it's only after firing that the true nature and colour of a glaze is revealed, so always label glaze containers.

KILNS, FIRING AND LOADING

Ten, twenty, thirty years ago, kilns were huge; that is to say thousands of bricks, stoke holes, chimneys and roaring wood fires, but nowadays they can

Kilns come in all shapes and sizes, but we reckon that if you are a beginner you can't beat a small electric kiln that has an automatic heat controller and cut-out. When you visit a supplier, make sure that you have a sketch plan of your workshop, showing areas, power points, door swing etc.

be pretty straightforward. They come in all shapes and sizes and you can walk into a showroom and buy one to suit your pocket and situation. There are small gas kilns, beautiful electric portables, lightweight fibre-lined top loaders and so on. However if you are a beginner go for an electric kiln with an automatic cut-out and think carefully before you settle for a particular model and type — have a good look through a supplier's catalogue, ask advice, talk to potters, visit schools, etc. Finally, when you visit a supplier take along a sketch plan showing preferred door swing distance, from power supply, etc.

Biscuit firing   Take all your dry, 'chalky' pots and place them in the kiln, largest and strongest at the bottom, and smallest and finest at the top. With a biscuit firing, pots can touch each other and the sides of the kiln, (not the elements), but just make sure that all the weights are evenly distributed. Once you are happy with the packing, set the kiln control at 'Low', open the spyhole vent, and leave the kiln overnight to 'steam' or 'smoke'. When the kiln temperature reaches 120–125°C, slowly take the temperature up to 500–600°C and then programme the kiln to go up to the recommended biscuit temperature, of say around 1000°C. With biscuit firing, most beginners tend to try and force the pace, so they rush the firing and the cooling, and unfortunately in both cases pots go bang. The golden rule of firings, and especially biscuit firing is, 'slowly to heat and slowly to cool'.

Glaze firing   Take your biscuit-fired and glaze-covered pots and very carefully pack them into the kiln, making sure that they are at least ¼ inch clear of each other and either have glaze-free bottoms, or are kept clear of the kiln shelf by being placed on little spurs, buttons or stands. Remember, as the glaze melts, so it runs like hot toffee; if pots touch each other or the sides of

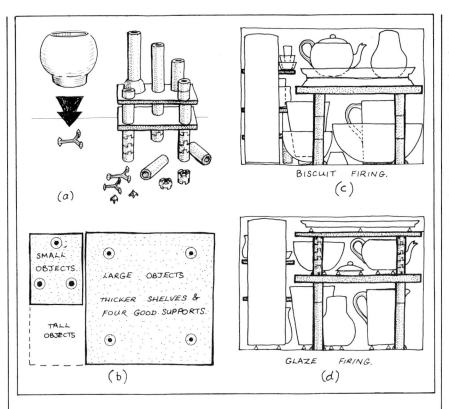

(a)

SMALL OBJECTS

LARGE OBJECTS

THICKER SHELVES & FOUR GOOD SUPPORTS.

TALL OBJECTS

(b)

BISCUIT FIRING.

(c)

GLAZE FIRING.

(d)

(a) When you buy your kiln make sure you get shelves of the correct size and a full range of kiln furniture. (b) See how it is possible to pack the kiln with all sizes of pots — use a variety of shelves and build up the levels independently (c) Biscuit kilns can be packed quite quickly; place big strong pots at the bottom, and fragile pots at the top — note how in a biscuit firing, pots can touch each other and the sides of the kiln (d) with a glaze firing the pots must either be wiped free from glaze, or supported on spurs — on no account must pots touch each other, the shelves, or the sides of the kiln.

the kiln, you will need a hammer and chisel to get them out of the kiln. Start the kiln packing from the bottom back, and gradually work forwards and upwards, trying along the way to fill every little space. Packing for a glaze firing is a slow and tricky task, because you might have to fiddle about for hours before you get the whole 'stilt, prop, shelf and pot' puzzle just right. When the glaze kiln is packed, set the control for 'Low', leave it a couple of hours for the glaze to dry out, then replace the spyhole/bung cover, and set the kiln to go up to, and cut out at, the glaze temperature. Of course you can't mix earthenware and stoneware glaze firings — if in doubt, refer to the kiln and glaze suppliers data sheets. And most important of all keep a kiln log of all firings then you will be able to build up your own individual data facts.

JAPANESE RAKU TEA-BOWLS

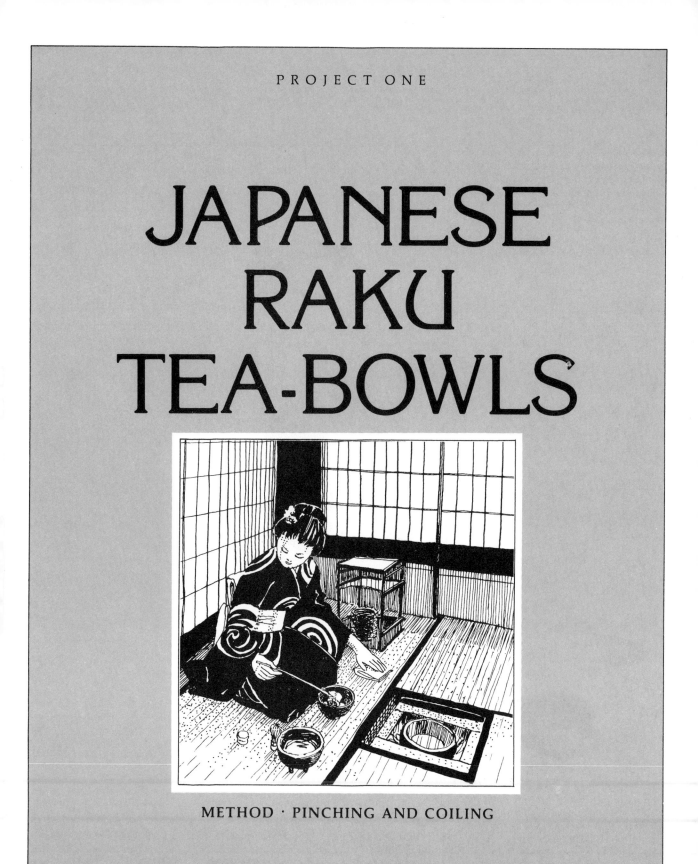

METHOD · PINCHING AND COILING

Working Drawing design grid. The scale is two grid squares to one inch. See how the Raku bowl is quite modest with a delicate foot ring and a half-glazed exterior. Note the irregular rim and the asymmetrical form.

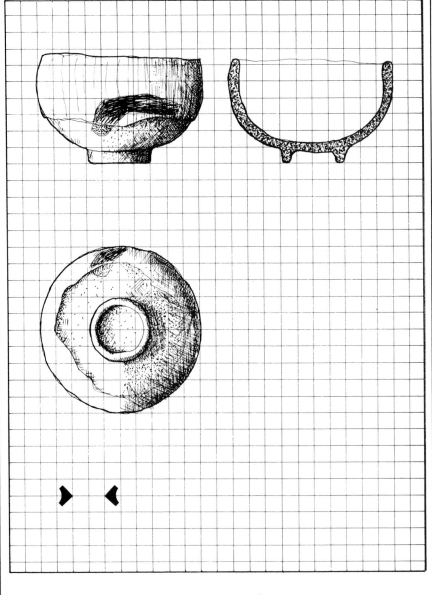

The finished bowl — get a clear picture in your mind's eye of how you want the bowl to be, then make detailed pencil sketches. Our bowl is very basic; that is to say it is made of Raku clay, it has a low temperature white glaze, and a decorative daub of black iron oxide.

INTRODUCTION

In Old Japan the Masters of the Tea ceremony took pleasure in using an austere, coarse, rather primitive, low-fired, soft-glazed ware that they called Raku. Traditionally Raku forms, usually small bowls, were biscuit fired —glazed — thrust into a charcoal fired kiln — snatched out with tongs when the glaze had melted, and then cooled and used . . . a sort of instant pottery experience! Although this basic type of pottery can now be made and worked in all manner of ways, it is generally accepted that Raku is still best pinched

Japanese Raku bowls and dishes have built in 'faults' — that is to say the glaze is heavy and dribbled, the clay body looks to be rather 'country', and there are variations in colour and texture. Of course we can't slavishly copy Raku bowls without knowing something of the Tea philosophy but we can use the Raku ware for design inspiration.

and coiled, lead glazed, and then fired at a low temperature of around 750°C. When we now talk of Raku ware, or Raku pottery, we usually mean any pottery or sculpture that is made from a coarse clay body and is able to withstand rapid changes in kiln temperature.

CONSIDERING THE PROJECT

TOOLS, EQUIPMENT AND MATERIALS

For this project you need a quantity of grogged grey Raku clay — a few ounces of black iron oxide — a handful of washed sand — a low temperature white Raku glaze, and the use of a small gas or electric kiln. And of course you will also need such workshop items as — a cutting wire, brushes, pencil and paper, cloths and various containers.

Before you actually start out on this project it might be as well to visit a museum and try to have a good close-up look at a few Japanese Raku bowls and dishes. See how the genuine article has built-in 'accidental' characteristics like glaze runs and dribbles, minute cracks, and variations in colour and texture. Finally when you have a clear picture in your mind's eye of just how you want your bowls to be, then you can make a few pencil sketches and set out your work area so that all your tools and materials are comfortably to hand.

PREPARING THE CLAY

WEDGING AND KNEADING

When you get your Raku clay from the supplier you will find, more often than not, that it is a rather bland, uniform and predictable product, so the first thing that you need to do is build-in a few unpredictable irregularities. Take a pinch or two of the black iron oxide and a handful of sand and dust them over your worksurface. Now take a manageable lump of clay, bang it down on the table, and then beat it with your palms until it looks like a large sharp ended loaf of bread. This done, take up the clay in 'praying' hands and smack it down on the table so that the sharp end is nearest you and tilted up. Now, in a single swift smooth movement, take the cutting wire and slide it

Spread a little iron oxide and sand over the worksurface, and wedge and knead the clay.

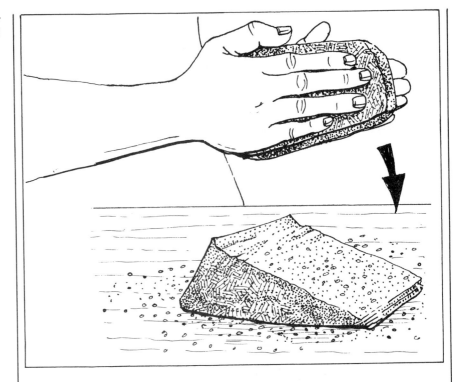

under and up, so that it cuts through the body of clay. Your long 'loaf' of clay should now be neatly cut in half — take the half nearest you, turn it round so that you can see the cut face, and then smack it down on its partner (see wedging in previous chapter).

Finally with open hands beat the clay back into the loaf shape. Repeat this wedging procedure four or five times until all the sand and iron oxide has been taken up and distributed evenly throughout the clay body. Now take the large lump of wedged clay — place it fair and square on the bench and with thumbs and fingers held together, knead it with a steady rhythmic 'down and away' action. Continue the kneading until the clay is nicely workable and free from lumps, bumps and air pockets.

FORMING THE THUMB-POT BASE

(MAKING SIX BOWLS)

Raku bowls are formed by a combination of two techniques: pinching, (sometimes called thumbing or thumb pinching), and coiling. Take six lumps of clay, each about as big as a small apple, and smack each piece into a smooth ball shape. Note — we like a set of bowls to vary just slightly in size and form, so we don't weigh out the clay; in our family we each have a bowl that suits our own individual size, needs and temperament; big, small, chubby, delicate and huge; we use them for soup and breakfast cereal. Now take the clay, ball at a time, press your thumb into its centre, and with a delicate pressing or squeezing action of thumb and fingers, form a shallow

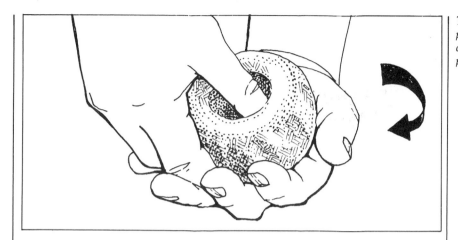

Take a small apple-sized ball of prepared clay, stick your thumb into its centre, and then shape it with a pinching action of thumb and fingers.

pinched dish. And so you continue — thumb pushing, turning, squeezing and shaping, until you have a foundation dish for each of the bowls that you want to make.

As each dish is made, check it over for faults and possible problems, and then cover it up with a damp cloth. Also from time to time, it's quite a good idea to look at the dishes as a group, and make size and form adjustments as you think fit.

COILING THE RIM AND FOOT

When you have made all the thumb-pinched bases and checked that they are similar in character, then you can start to build the bowls. Take a lump of clay and with out-stretched fingers roll it out on the workbench until you have

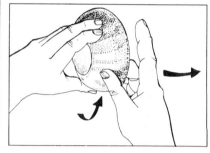

As the little pinch-pot begins to grow, shape it with a continuous turning and squeezing action.

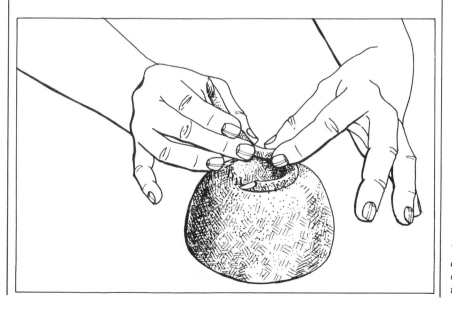

To make the bowl-foot, take a coil of clay, make a small ring, place the ring of clay on the upturned pot, and work it into the main body of the clay.

You can work up the sides of the thumb-pot by adding coils to the rim — keep the pot moving, and control and shape the form with a gentle pursuading action.

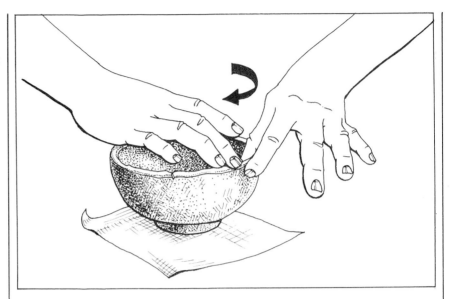

made a 'worm', or coil, that is about as thick as a pencil and free from lumps, bits and cracks. It is most important at this stage, that the clay stays soft and workable, so as you make the coils, place them under a damp cloth. Note — you should be able to wrap a coil of workable clay into a tight ring without it cracking or breaking up.

Now take one of the little dish bases and carefully place a coil of clay round its rim, then with thumb and fingers, work the added clay into the body of the dish. And so you continue adding coils until the bowl grows in height and diameter. If you want the bowl to grow out, then you add coils to the outside rim, and if you want the bowl sides to turn in, you add the coils to the inside rim.

If you are making more than one bowl, it's a good idea to work all the bowls in turn, coil by coil; it gives the clay a chance to stiffen and also ensures that the bowls grow and develop as a considered group. The coiling process is one of adding, squeezing, shaping and gently persuading. When you add the final coil, that is the bowl rim coil, give it extra time, and finger squeeze and smooth the rim and bring it to a fine rounded finish. Each bowl will need a foot or base ring; so turn the finished bowls upside down, position small rings or hoops of clay, as illustrated, and then with thumbs and fingers work them into the body of the clay.

DECORATION

When the bowls are almost dry, set them out on the worksurface; check them over for faults, cracks and the like; throw away any bowls that are less than beautiful; then arrange brushes, water, iron oxide etc so that they are comfortably to hand. Now make a little dish out of a pellet of clay and mix a small pinch of iron oxide with water until you have a smooth black slip. Use this 'paint' to brush-decorate your bowls with free pattern; go for flowers and simple restrained brush strokes rather than overworked subtle designs.

BISCUIT FIRING

When your bowls are dry, they can be fired to a biscuit temperature. Place the pots in the kiln, largest and strongest at the bottom, and lightest and most delicate at the top. Shut the kiln door, take out the bung and turn on the power. Aim to gradually build up the temperature over about six hours until it is around the 600–650°C mark. Finally, when the kiln contents have reached a dull red heat, turn off the power and let the pots cool down slowly.

GLAZING AND GLAZE FIRING

Weigh out a quantity of white Raku glaze, as directed by the manufacturer, and mix it with water until it is the consistency of single cream. Now take each of your biscuit fired bowls in turn, hold them by their base rings, and slide them swiftly in and out of the liquid glaze. Try and hold the bowls at an angle, as illustrated, then you can glaze both the inside and outside in a single, direct, uncomplicated operation. Note — In our opinion Raku bowls look better if the glaze line finishes well clear of the base ring; so leave the glaze line unwiped; then when the pot is fired, it will form a most beautiful roll or 'lip' of thick glaze. Finally, let the glazed pots dry out, and then return them to the kiln and fire them to a soft-glaze temperature of about 750–800°C.

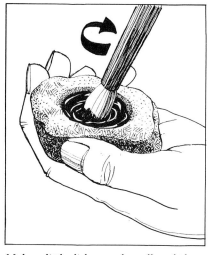

Make a little dish out of a pellet of clay, mix a smooth slip 'paint' with water and iron oxide, and use this 'paint' to decorate your bowls.

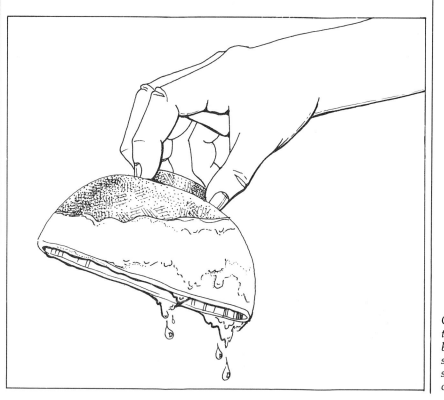

Once the bowl has been biscuit fired, then it needs to be glazed — hold the bowl, at an angle, by its foot ring, and slide it swiftly in and out of the glaze — see how the foot and an irregular part of the bowl is left unglazed.

HINTS, TIPS AND NOTES

Clay body mixes, glaze recipes, kiln temperature readings etc are all, to some extent, unpredictable; so be ready to adjust techniques and methods. If, as you are working, your clay becomes a little stiff, leave it in a plastic bag with a damp cloth — never wet it directly.

Glaze mixtures are best kept in lidded plastic bowls and buckets; keep the glaze area clean, and stir the glaze before use. If you make a mess-up of the glaze dipping, don't fiddle and fuss around; just wash the pot, let it dry, and then leave it for another day. As the base or foot rings of Raku pots are left unglazed, they can sit directly on kiln shelves; you don't have to worry about stilts, kiln furniture and the like.

'ARTS AND CRAFTS' OWL

METHOD · PINCHING, COILING AND MODELLING

Working drawing design grid — the scale is two grid squares to one inch. See how the owl is about ten inches high and five inches wide. Note also the loose fitting lid/head and the decorative tile feather feature.

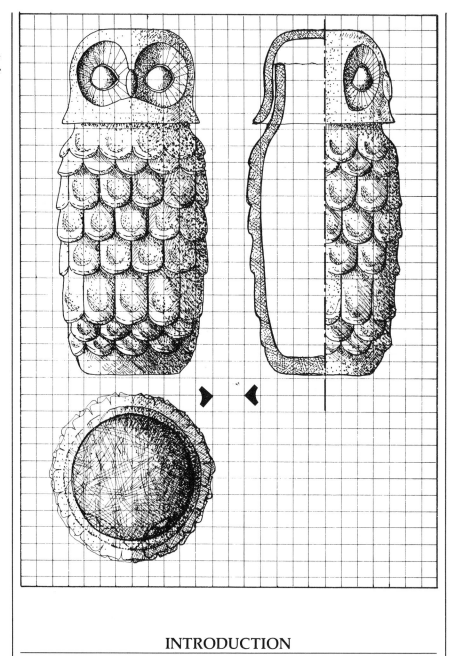

INTRODUCTION

The 'Arts and Crafts' movement started in Britain in the last quarter of the nineteenth century when for the first time artists and craftsmen came together in an attempt to 'enrich the industrial arts'. Artist-potters, inspired by new forms, glazes and techniques, decided that they wanted to step outside the factory-made pottery tradition and both design and make their own wares in

Inspirational — Owl forms have always been a favourite with potters, and as you can see they come in all shapes and sizes — so if you want to adjust this project, there is no reason at all why you should not change the owl type and make it bigger, smaller or whatever.

individual pottery studios. Of course this first generation of artist-potters couldn't, at a stroke, get back to the rural folk-art traditions; but they did set the pace for all that was to follow — Art School ceramics; children's pottery in schools; evening class pottery groups and hobby ceramics. For us the pinched and coiled Owl says it all — OK, so it's not especially beautiful; nor is it necessarily good in the sense of being highbrow pottery with a capital P, but it is evocative of a first pottery making experience.

CONSIDERING THE PROJECT

TOOLS EQUIPMENT AND MATERIALS

For this project you need a pound or two of red or grey earthenware clay; a coloured earthenware 'art' glaze; say a good rich red or maybe a honey; the use of a small kiln, (gas or electric makes no difference), and such tools as a banding wheel, a cutting wire, a wire scoop-tool, glaze sticks, a needle pricker, stick modelling tools, pencil and paper, jugs, cloths and the like.

In many ways this project is ideal for beginners because not only are all the individual stages of construction easy to manage, but the end result is quite impressive. Have a good look at our inspirational illustrations and working drawings and study just how the Owl lidded pot/sculpture is put together. See how it is made-up out of three pots; two for the body, and one for the lid; and how the feather texture is built up from rows of carefully considered tiles or pellets of clay. And of course before you set out on this pottery adventure, visit museums, galleries and the like, and see if you can sketch and study owl profiles and characteristics. It might also be a good idea to take picture clips from old magazines — birds, feathers, beaks and such like. Note — if you can, search out 'bird' vases of the 1890–1930 period, eg 'Owl' pieces made by the Martin brothers, Southall, London circa 1899.

FIRST STEPS

With a pinched, coiled and modelled project of this size, type and character, it is most important that the small amount of clay that you are going to use is well prepared and in a good workable state. Spend time wedging and kneading, and make sure the clay is smooth textured and free from lumps of hard clay and air pockets. If you look at the working drawings, you will see that we have chosen to make rather a serious looking owl that is about ten inches high and five inches wide, but of course there is no reason at all why you shouldn't make one that is double the size; say twenty or thirty inches high or even one that is really very small — think on it, and make a few design sketches. Take your prepared clay, cut off four large apple sized lumps and put them under a damp cloth; wipe down your worksurface and then arrange your tools so that they are close at hand.

MAKING THE BASIC BODY FORM

Take a ball of clay, thrust your thumb into its centre and then by revolving the ball on your thumb and at the same time squeezing the clay between thumb and fingers, set about making a classic cup shaped pinch or thumb pot. Make two identical pots. It's a good idea to build both pots at the same time; working a few minutes on the first pot; then on the second; and then back to the first — in this way you will finish up with two similar and balanced forms. If you are new to pottery making, there will, no doubt, be a certain amount of trial, error and experimentations but don't lose heart; battle on until you have achieved two identical deep cup-shaped bowls. Note — try, if possible, to keep the thumb-pots 'tight', that is, don't let them spread or let the rim flop over.

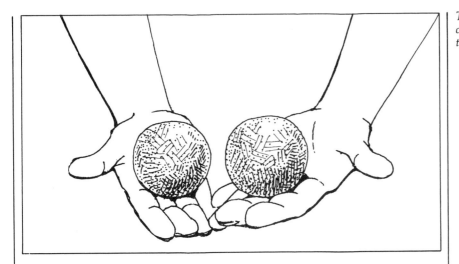

Take two identical balls of prepared clay and set about making two pinched thumb-pots.

The next step can be a little tricky, so go at it very gently and take your time. Smooth and level up the rims of both pots so that they can be brought together to make a nice fit. Now carefully place the two pots rim-to-rim and then go round the seam 'thumbing' the clay up and down, and from pot-to-pot until the join disappears. This done roll out a long fat coil of clay, wrap it round the seam and then work it into the main body of the pot until the join is well and truly welded and the overall form firmly established. And so you continue, smearing, turning, and smoothing until you have in your hands a well shaped fat 'egg' or ovoid. Once you have achieved this form, and you are sure that it is well jointed and completely air-tight, you can start to shape and model the owl characteristics.

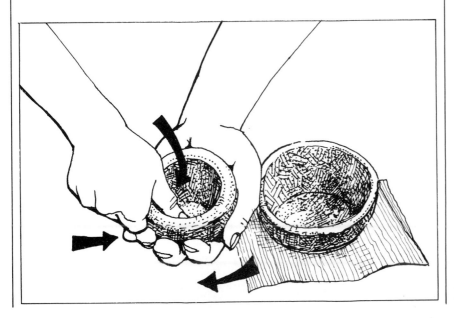

Work the two pots so that, as near as possible, they are the same diameter and depth.

*Take the two pinched thumb-pots and
join them rim to rim — weld the joint
with a coil of clay.*

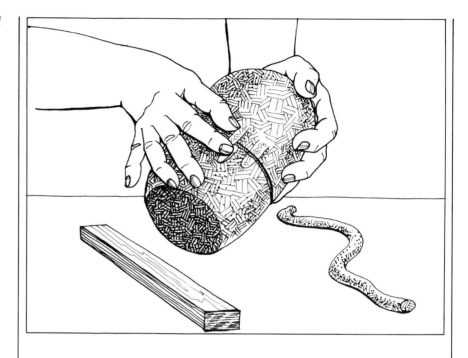

SHAPING THE OWL BODY

Cradle the hollow 'egg' of clay in your hands and feel out its weight and
potential; then have another look at your sketches and working drawings
and then get to work. The shaping is best managed by an almost continuous
hand action of turning and beating, and so you work: turning and tapping,
turning and tapping; until the 'egg' begins to grow into an elongated gourd
shape. Note — as long as the hollow form is air-tight and you don't lose
control and hit it too hard you can beat it into whatever shape takes your
fancy.

When you have achieved a satisfactory form, tap it at one end so that it sits
on a good firm base; pierce it at the top with a pin; and then let it dry until it is
firm but still workable. Now take the looped wire tool and cut an opening
where you want the owl's neck to be. Finally take a scrap of clay, roll it into a
coil and then build up the neck opening until it is well formed and slightly
tapered. This done, cover the body shape with plastic film so that the clay
stays plastic and workable.

MAKING THE OWL HEAD

Take one of the remaining balls of clay, and make another pinch pot as
already described; but this time build a lid/head that sits on and over the
owl's neck. When you have made the head to a good loose fit, then you can
start to model and shape the form. You might have deep dished eye hollows;
applied pellets of clay for the eyes and beak; texture for the feathers or
whatever — see the working drawings and design sketches.

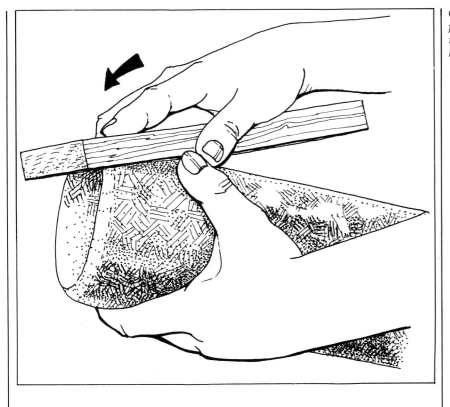

Once you have made a large 'egg' by joining the two pots, and you are sure that it is air-tight, take a batten and beat and shape the owl's body.

MODELLING THE FORM

You should now have two main sculptural elements, a tall bottle-shaped body with a slender neck and a loose fitting dome shaped lid/head. Fit the two together, trimming to fit, then go back to your working drawings, sketches and magazine clips.

If you look at our project, as illustrated, you will see that we haven't attempted to make a realistic owl; but rather we have taken the main characteristics and built them into a stylized and simplified form. See how the 'feathers' are built up like roof tiles or shingles and how they are organized into a series of over-lapping rows. Of course there is no need to slavishly copy our style; you might want the tiles to be rather more delicate; or smaller, larger, thinner or the like. Have a trial run with some scrap clay and see if you can come up with some interesting variations on the applied 'tile' theme. When you come to the modelling of all the little tiles and tabs, you need to work in a well organized and considered fashion; that is you must make sure the body of the pot is slightly moist and still workable; you must give yourself banded guide lines to work to; and you must build little stock-piles of, graded to size, tiles.

Fix the tiles row by row starting at the bottom of the pot and fix them to the main body of the pot with a positive thumb-smearing action. Make sure the tiles are in a staggered sequence and make sure that each row is well fixed

Once you have achieved a form with a base and a necked rim, measure and set-out the position of the tile feathers — see how the tiles are modelled like roof tiles, that is in overlapping rows.

When you come to making the head/lid, make a small pinch pot, as already described; make it to fit the neck rim, and then model the eye hollows.

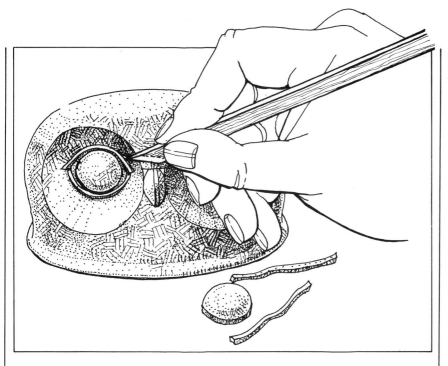

Finally, model the head with eye and beak additions — use small pellets and coils of clay and use a stick-tool.

before you go onto the next. This may all sound incredibly finger twisting but in fact it is really straightforward. And so you continue building up the stylized plumage.

If you look at our owl, as illustrated, you will see that we have stopped the 'tiles' just short of the shoulder line; but you could go on and say, cover the head with feathers, build out a suggestion of wings, model a fantastic head-crest. However when you consider the owl finished let it dry out very slowly in a well aired room.

BISCUIT FIRING

When the owl sculpture/vase is completely dry; that is you can scratch it and leave a 'chalky' mark, then it needs to be biscuit fired. Before you actually close the door of the kiln on the owl, give it one last checking over and make sure that all is correct. Fire the kiln to a low biscuit temperature of around 850–900°C — take the temperature up very slowly, say 0–600°C overnight, (with the bung or spyhole open), then programme the kiln to cut out at about 900°C. Note — with a biscuit firing all the pots in the kiln are unglazed, so they can touch each other and the sides of the kiln.

GLAZING

Brush down your biscuit fired owl and make sure that it is free from dust, scraps of fired clay and greasy finger marks; then arrange the bucket of glaze and the various sticks, jugs, cloths and sponges so that they are at hand.

Start by taking a jug full of well stirred glaze and washing out the inside of the owl, body and lid, fill the owl body with glaze and then with a rotating action, empty the glaze back into the bucket. When both the owl's body and head have been glazed on the inside you can glaze them on the outside. Place a couple of sticks across a wide bowl; carefully position the body of the owl, rim down, and then, working with care and swiftness, cover it with jug-poured glaze. Repeat this with the owl head/lid. Don't labour the glaze pouring; just get it done as quickly as possible and aim to cover the owl with an even thin coat. Finally, when the two elements are dry, pick them up with crisp-dry fingers and very carefully sponge-wipe the glaze off the body base and the lid rim.

GLAZE FIRING

Take the two glazed and wiped items, and using stilts or spurs set them up on the kiln shelf. Note — because you have wiped the base and rim clear of glaze you could, if you so wish, stand them on the shelf directly. When you are sure that all is correct, very gently shut the kiln door, leave the bung open and then turn on the power. Aim to raise the kiln temperature slowly for the first hour; just to let the glaze dry out; then turn the heat straight up and programme the kiln to cut-out at the recommended glaze temperature — say around 1020–1100°C.

HINTS, TIPS AND NOTES

With a sculptural, built-up and modelled pot of this character you do have to watch out that the clay remains workable; so between stages keep it covered with plastic film.

When you come to the initial drying out, prior to the biscuit firing, make sure the pot is protected from draughts, blasts of hot air from central heating blowers and direct sunlight.

If you are short of kiln space and you want to glaze fire the owl with the lid in position, make sure that the inside of the lid and all other points of contact are free from glaze. If you find that the poured glaze hasn't quiet covered, and say missed a feather tip or 'tile' overhang, dab it with a glaze loaded brush.

PERUVIAN SPOUTED CAT VASE

METHOD · PINCHING, COILING AND MODELLING

Working drawing design grid — the scale is one grid square to one inch — the cat is about 12 inches from nose to tail, and 13 inches from the base to the top of the spout. Note the integral spout/handle and the air-flow control hole in the handle.

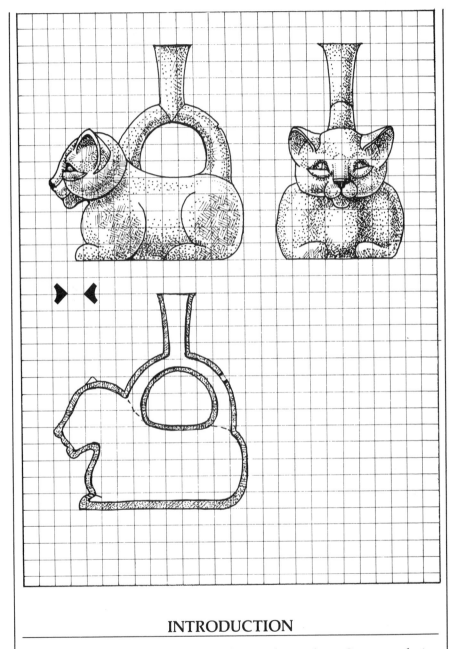

INTRODUCTION

The Mochica and Nazca pottery making Indians of pre-Conquestadorian Peru have been described as 'portrait and effigy mastercraftsmen'. Not for these potters simple domestic mugs, jugs and bowls, but rather they concentrated their efforts on making and modelling all manner of beautifully built, stirrup-handled and spouted, sculptural forms. Effigy vases showing priests and soldiers; modelled pots showing men and women at work and

Inspirational — Nazca effigy vase — the head, spout and handle are all worked so that there is a nicely controlled flow when pouring water — this pot is burnished to a high shine.

play; and best of all, wonderfully constructed and fantastically designed, painted and spouted sculptural vases in the form of birds, faces, snakes and animals. These pots characteristically all have bold graphic motifs worked in white, black and red; double and single integral spout-handles, and high-shine polished haematite surfaces. The Mochica and Nazca artist-sculptors achieved all this by the very simplest means; no wheels, glazes or high temperature kilns; just a unique understanding and use of the basic pottery techniques of coiling, pinching, modelling and burnishing.

CONSIDERING THE PROJECT

TECHNIQUES, TOOLS AND MATERIALS

If you are a beginner to pottery, with a minimum of tools equipment and space, and are also interested in sculptural forms; rather than say domestic thrown pottery; this could well be the project for you. Before you consider putting hands to clay, start by having a good look at our working drawings and inspirational illustrations, and then, if possible, visit a museum that has a 'primitive' pottery collection. Search out examples of Middle and South American pre-European Indian pottery, and then stop awhile and study form, construction and decorative style. See how the burnished earthenware

Inspirational – Peruvian spouted figure vase – portrait vases of this character all look to be modelled from life.

pots tend to be gourd-like in shape, and how the slip decorated and stylized motifs are worked and placed. Lastly find out as much as you can about the texture of the clay body by looking at pottery sherds and then make some detailed sketches of characteristic motifs, patterns and designs. Finally, when you feel that you understand just what it is that goes to make a coiled and modelled 'primitive' pot, get down to work.

For this project you need a quantity of well sanded, red earthenware clay, white and red slip, a few ounces of black iron oxide, a little powdered haematite, a few stick modelling tools, and such workshop items as, brushes, mixing bowls, pencil and paper; and of course you will need the use of a low temperature gas or electric kiln.

FIRST STEPS

THE PINCH POT

Take three or four good sized lumps of prepared and workable clay; cover them with a moist cloth and then set out your tools and materials so that they are within reach. This done, take a large apple-sized lump of clay, smack it into a ball, and thrust the thumb of your right hand into its centre. Now support the clay in your cupped left hand and then gently work it with a squeezing action of thumb-pad and finger tips. As the clay is pivotted and squeezed, work it so that it gradually grows into a thumb-pot or pinch-pot form, (see also other projects). Work with an easy rhythm and at a comfortable pace; all the time making sure that the bowl's growth is stable and controlled. And so you continue, adjusting the form, smoothing and repairing puckers and rim cracks, and generally keeping the bowl's growth

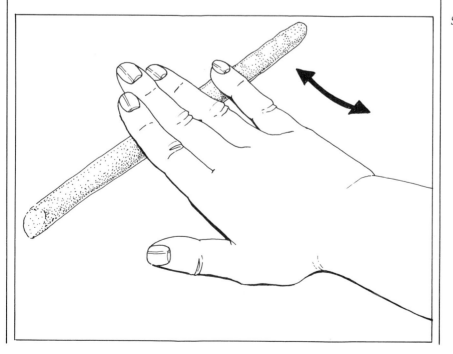

Start by rolling out a stock-pile of coils.

and shape in check. Note — if you are making the cat, rather than say a bird or whatever, then the basic pinch-pot foundation needs to be round ended and boat-like.

COILING UP

When you have achieved a well formed base and related it to your working drawings, you can start to coil and model. Take a small lump of clay and with outstretched fingers, as illustrated, roll it out on the workbench and make a slender pencil-thick coil. Now take the boat shaped base, place the coil of clay round its rim, and then thumb-smear the added clay into the main body of the base. And so you work, adding coil upon coil until the base grows in height and form. When you want the form to 'belly out', add the coils to the rim and thumb-smear, as described, but this time instead of trying to keep the clay walls upright, squeeze and ease the coiled additions 'over-and-out'. And of course when you want the growing form to narrow or 'neck-in', then you ease the added clay 'over and in'. And so you work, checking and double checking the working drawings, adding coils of clay, and all the while pinching, squeezing, adjusting and modelling the clay to suit.

Coil up from a pinch-pot base, try to keep the form tight and controlled, don't let the rim flop over or weaken.

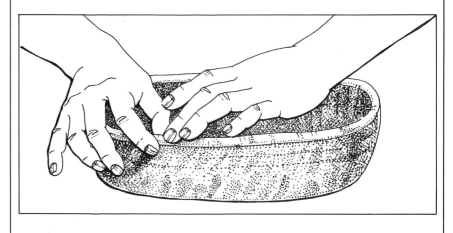

COILING AND MODELLING THE CAT HEAD

When you have built-up and worked the cat form and say coiled and modelled the haunches, shoulders etc you need to start on the head. Work and coil the chest out; using clay props to support the chin overhang; then, when the clay has stiffened, coil and model the nose, cheeks and the back of the head. Now this part of the project is tricky because the clay at the neck has to be soft enough to work, but at the same time it needs to be stiff enough to take the weight of the head, so build up with care and make sure that you keep the shell of clay, thin, rounded and free from cracks and flaws. Note — when you are working the chin 'out-and-up' it is a good idea to build in temporary clay chin-chest supports, as illustrated, and cut them out at a later stage.

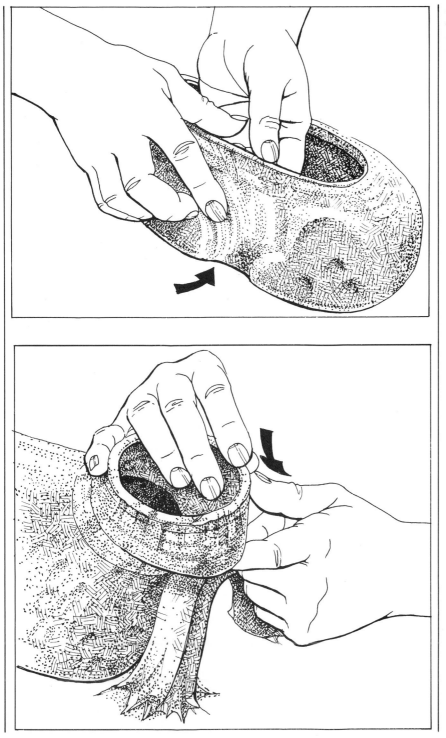

Gradually coil in, and at the same time, working with say your fingers and a rubber kidney tool, press out and model the haunches and the shoulders.

When you come to making the head, support the chin overhang with clay props, and try, if possible, to control the clay drying so that the neck and base become firm enough to take the added weight.

The spout/handle needs to spring out of the body of the cat in a smooth curve, — see how the weight of the handle is supported by a temporary clay armature or gantry.

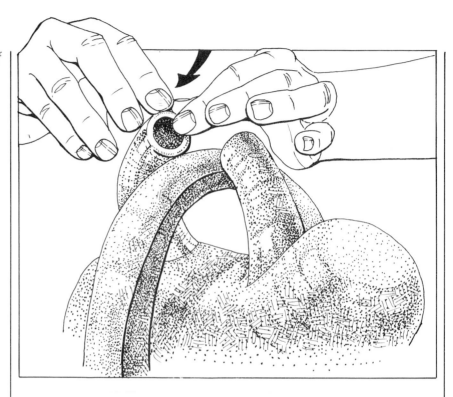

COILING THE SPOUTED HANDLE

If you look at our working drawings and illustrations and your sketches etc, you will see that the spout/handle is in effect a hollow tubed addition that grows up out of the cat's neck and rump in a smooth curve. Let the main shell of clay dry out until it is firm, but still workable, then close up the cat's back, as illustrated. Your cat sculpture should now be rounded and enclosed, apart that is, from the two spout holes. Work both holes up into little necked rims, and model and curve as you go. Aim to work on both holes alternately, building a coil each at a time. If you reach a point when you reckon that the weight of the clay at the spout is too much for the still damp clay of the cat's back, then build a temporary clay armature or gantry that bridges the cat's back and takes the weight. Continue coiling the two spouts so that they curve towards each other and come together in a smooth modelled and tubed arch. This done, cut into the arch at its proudest point and coil up until you can bring the spout, come handle, to a smooth, necked and slightly flared finish.

When you consider the overall sculptural form well worked and structurally sound, let it dry a little; go over it with a wood, metal or rubber kidney tool, and model and consolidate the clay at the various curves, bulges, creases and overhangs. Finally, build out, coil and model the details of the nose, ears, eyes etc.

DECORATION

When your cat sculpture is at the leather-hard stage, set it up on the workbench and have the slips, black iron oxide, red haematite, brushes and

Inspirational — traditional Peruvian border repeats, worked in red, white and black slips.

Inspirational – Nazca vase worked in red, white and brown slips – the reptilian motifs are in the form of an interlocking repeat.

mixing bowls at the ready. Take three bowls and put some brown slip in one and white slip in the other two. Now take the dish of brown slip, add to it a little black iron oxide, and then mix it to a smooth, creamy, black, lump-free 'paint'. This done, take up one of the two bowls of white slip, add a pinch or two of red haematite, and mix it also to a smooth 'paint'.

You should now have three slip/oxide colours in all, white, black and red. Note — these slip 'paints' need to be thick but at the same time, they must be completely free from lumps of unmixed oxide powder. Ideally a slip paint should be dense in colour; thick; smooth; creamy; non-runny and well stirred.

Now for the actual decorating; before you put brush to clay, go back to your work drawings, sketches and photographs and see just how the lines of the designs, motifs and patterns are organized. Note how some patterns are say white on red, and others are multi-coloured with hard-edged black outlines. It might also be a good idea, at this stage, to make a few more pencil sketches and have some trial 'dry runs' on some scrap clay. This done, mark out the lines of the design on the leather-hard clay and delicately edge them in with a shallow-cut incised line. Finally, when the design has been set out, carefully block-in and paint the various areas of the motifs with two coats of thick coloured slip.

BURNISHING

When the slip painted designs are set and non tacky, and the ground clay is well past the leather-hard stage, you can get down to the pleasuresome business of burnishing, or rubbing and polishing the clay. With the leather-

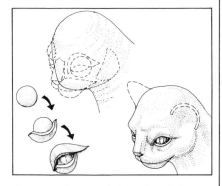

Once you have coiled up the whole form, start to add small pellets and coils of clay, and model the fine delicate features.

hard cat in one hand and a metal spoon or wooden tool in the other, set about burnishing the clay with a firm polishing and pressing action; aim to take the surface to a slightly dappled, high-shine finish. Note — if when you are burnishing, the clay surface looks to be 'chalky', or in any way powdery, it is possible that the clay is too dry; it is most important that you catch the clay at just the right stage.

FIRING

Take your pinched, coiled, slip and oxide decorated, burnished sculpture/pot and, making sure that it is totally dry, place it in a biscuit kiln. Take the temperature of the kiln up very slowly, say 0–600°C over an eight hour period, and then set the controls to cut-out at about 800–850°C. Finally, when the pot is just cool enough to handle, give it a good daubing with either butter or wax, a thorough polishing with a brush and cloth, and the job is done.

HINTS, TIPS AND NOTES

Coiling and modelling a sculptural pot of this size, type and character is fraught with difficulties, not the least of these being that the building needs to be slow and spread out over hours, days and weeks; there is no 'easy' sure-fire 'quick' method; just be patient and prepared for a deal of sitting, waiting and watching.

When you come to mixing the slip paints, white, red and black, it is possible to broaden your palette by mixing and grading all the colours. So you might mix, reddish white, pink, red, reddish black, black, grey and all the colours and tones in between. However, aim to keep the motifs bold, direct, hard edged and as simple as possible.

With a complex hand-built sculpture of this size, type and character it is most important that the drying out be slow; so avoid direct sunlight, blasts of hot air and draughts.

If you decide to build a clay gantry to take the weight of the spouted handle, cut it out well before the handle/spout starts to dry and shrink. If the kiln temperature goes much above 850°C the haematite colour and the burnished polish will burn out, so best keep the temperature below 900°C. If you decide to pad out with newspaper during the 'making' stage, don't worry about removing the paper before firing; leave the paper be, and let it burn away.

A low temperature, unglazed pot of this character won't hold water in the sense that it could be stood on top of the telly or on a polished surface. When you build on the little coiled and modelled details like ears, eyes etc, make sure that you don't trap pockets of air; pierce possible problem areas with a fine needle.

AFRICAN TRIBAL POT

METHOD · HAND-BUILDING, COILING AND MODELLING

Working drawing design grid – the scale is one grid square to one inch. The pot measures about 12 inches across the belly, about 12 inches across the mouth, and is 13–14 inches in total height. This particular pot is totally round bottomed and designed to sit in a quoit, but you could, if you wish, adjust the design slightly and make a pot with a flat base or a foot ring.

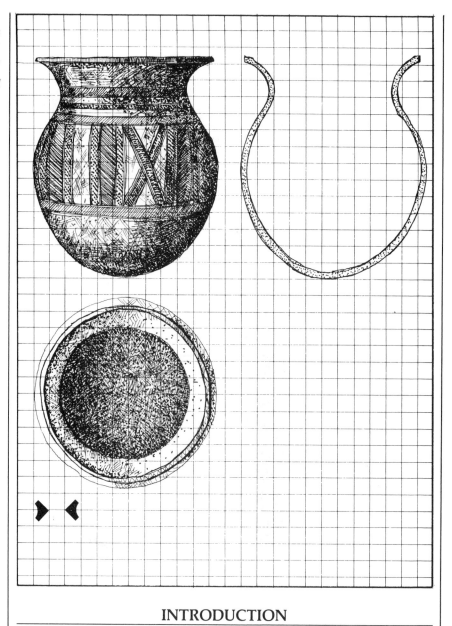

INTRODUCTION

Giant water vessels, beautifully worked bowls, dishes and food containers and whole villages all built of clay; no this isn't an exaggerated account of wild imaginings; this is how it is now in many traditional African tribal societies. The African village potters, usually women, create the most wonderful pottery forms using only the simpliest of tools; no kilns, no glazes and no wheels; just a total understanding of the properties of locally dug clay and the social and economic need to make functional domestic pottery ware.

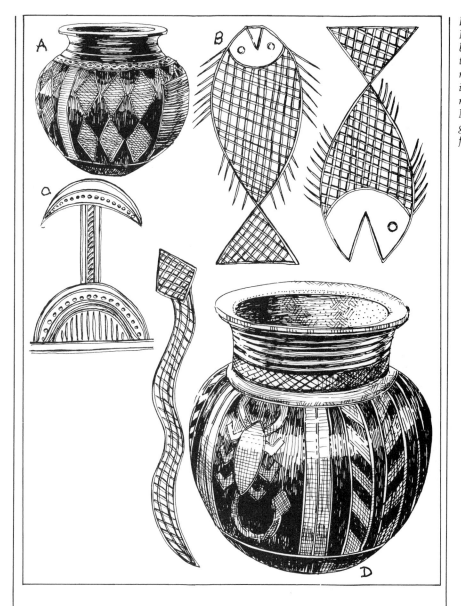

Inspirational — (a) a traditional Nigerian form with incised design of bordered geometrical motifs (b) a traditional Nigerian fish and snake motif (c) a small motif worked with incised cuts and pressed dots (d) a modern Nigerian pot made in Abuja Nigeria — although this pot has been glazed, it still uses traditional decorative forms and motifs.

African pottery tends to be round-based, flare necked, hand-built and unglazed; the shapes and forms being determined by usage, function, materials and building techniques. The African village houses are basic, with uneven floors, and few, if any, flat surfaces; so what better than having round based pots that nestle in hollows on the ground, or flare necked vessels that are hung in a sling? And of course as there are no polished surfaces, only the need to keep foods cool, what could be more suitable than low fired porous earthenware with its own in-built, self regulating, water evaporation cooling system?

It is not possible for us to describe each and every tribal method of pot building, because of course there are many different traditions and techniques, but perhaps they can all be summed up as being hand-built; that is, slabbed, coiled and to some extent moulded. Generally speaking African women potters build their pots directly out of a hollow in the ground, or up from a 'broken pot' mould. Coarse, well grogged clay is fist pummelled or heel-pushed into a concave mould, or sometimes over a hump mould, and then the rest of the pot is built up with thick wads, coils or slugs of clay.

The potter works, walks, and moves round the pot, adding, coiling, smoothing and shaping as she goes. This done, the big bold spherical pots are decorated with incised lines and ochres, allowed to dry slightly, and then burnished. Finally the dry pots are heaped up in a village 'kiln'; That is a pile of pots about 3 feet high and 10 feet across; covered with twigs, grass and corn stalks; and then fired to a dull red heat of about 650–850°C. When the fired pots are taken from the kiln embers, they are rubbed with waxy leaf and animal fat mixtures and then polished to a high shine.

CONSIDERING THE PROJECT

TOOLS, EQUIPMENT AND MATERIALS

We have chosen to work this project in the West African Vume tradition; that is we build and coil up a domed half-pot, and then turn it over and coil up from the belly rim. However there is no reason at all why you shouldn't work to another tradition and say build a slab base in a concave mould and then coil up; or maybe build a slab base over a hump mould; let it dry, flip it over, and then coil up.

There are a great many traditional African methods and styles of pottery building, so before you start out on this project, stop awhile and consider the various possibilities. Do you, for example, have a large plaster mould? How big do you want your pot to be? Are you strong enough to 'flip' a half made bowl over when it might weigh ten or so pounds? and so on. Finally when you

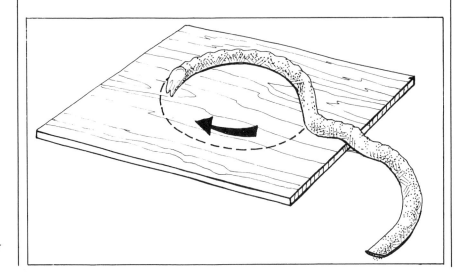

Start by setting out a 12 inch diameter base coil.

have a clear picture in your mind's eye of how you want the pot to be and how you want it to be built, go to a library, visit a museum, look at as many examples of African pottery as you can find, and then start sketching and collecting inspirational material.

For this project you need about 25 lbs of red earthenware clay, about 7 lbs of fine-ground grog, ½ lb of black iron oxide, a quantity of brown slip, a large wooden working board; a piece of ¾ inch plywood 18 × 18 inches will do just fine, the use of a good strong stable workbench, the use of a gas or electric kiln, and of course such general workshop items as, sponges, plastic containers, stick-tools, a cutting wire, brushes, a wooden beater, a metal kidney, and plastic sheeting.

FIRST STEPS

GROGGING, WEDGING AND KNEADING

Clear the worksurface and have your clay, grog and cutting wire to hand. First dust a handful of grog over the bench; then take a large manageable lump of clay and smack it down on the grogged surface. This done, slice the clay with the cutting wire (½ inch thick slices), dust each slice with grog, then start to pull the clay together. Beat and pummel the whole heap with your palms until it begins to look rather like a sharp-ended, rough textured loaf of bread. So far so good; now lift up the clay in 'praying' hands and smash it down on the table so that its sharp end is tilted up towards you. Now take the taut thumb-pressed cutting wire, and push it 'under-and-up' through the clay so that the 'loaf' is neatly halved. This done, take the half nearest you, turn it round so that you can see the cut face, and then smash it down on its other half. And so you continue, dusting, cutting, smashing and wedging, until allthe grog is evenly distributed throughout the clay body.

Build, coil and model up from the base ring, and bring the form to a well curved and rimmed finish.

Finally take the wedged clay, cut it into manageable lumps and then with a steady hand-pushing, 'down-and-away' action knead it until it is workable, even-textured and free from lumps of hard clay and air pockets.

BUILDING AND COILING THE NECKED HALF-POT

Wipe and brush down your worksurface, set out your workboard, cover your grogged and wedged clay with a moist cloth, and then arrange your working area so that all the tools are within reach. Now have a good long look at your various notes, magazine clips and inspirational drawings, and then to work.

First take the compasses and set out the workboard with a 12 inch diameter circle. This done, cut off half a dozen apple-sized balls of clay, and with straight outstretched fingers roll out a stock-pile of sausage-thick coils or slugs. Note — when you have rolled out a supply of coils, don't let them dry; cover them up with a damp cloth or fine plastic sheet.

When you are coiling, keep the base ring workable by covering it with a plastic sheet — the upper half of the pot needs to be about 7–8 inches high, about 7 inches at the neck, and 11 inches at the rim.

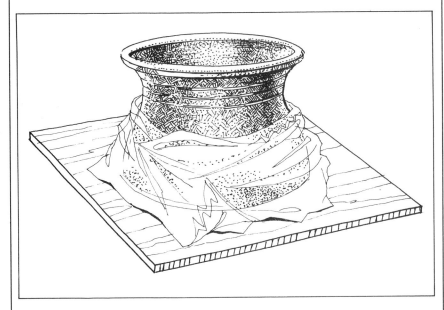

Now, using the board and the 12 inch diameter circle as your base-line, lay down a thick coiled ring of clay, as illustrated. Continue adding, coil upon coil, and thumb-smearing the additions so that the pot form grows, dome-like up and in. When the dome is about 5–6 inches high and the mouth hole about 7–8 inches across, change tack, and build and work the coils so that they flare out to a nicely curved trumpet-shaped rim. When you reckon that the half-pot looks about right, take the metal kidney scraper and move, work and consolidate the coiled form so that its lines are smooth and considered, and its structure stable and free from joins, breaks, cracks and flaws. Finally, cover the lower section of the half-pot with thin plastic sheeting, as illustrated, and let the neck rim dry out and stiffen.

COILING UP THE BASE

When the necked half-pot is stiff enough to take its own weight, slice it off the workboard with the taut thumb-pressed wire; then, holding and supporting both the board and the half-pot, flip the whole arrangement over, and remove the board. You should now have a half-pot that is sitting upside down on its own finished neck — a sort of open bottomed bowl. Now pare

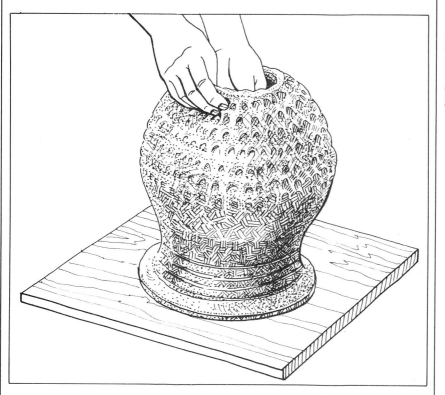

When the necked half-pot is stiff enough to take its own weight, slice it off the workboard, turn it over, and then coil up from the initial 12 inch belly coil. Gradually bring the coils up and in, and aim for a smooth domed form.

down the rim, or what was your initial board coil, and then continue to coil, build and 'dome-up', as before. This time however, continue building until the dome or the base-to-be is closed and covered in. Finally, when the last coil is in place, take the small wooden beater and smack and shape the dome so that its form is smooth-curved and symmetrical.

FINISHING, SCRAPING AND DECORATING

When the whole pot is soft leather-hard, turn it right side up, and cradle it in your lap or on a small plastic bowl. Now take the metal kidney-shaped scraper and work the inside of the pot until it is smooth-curved and somewhat reduced in weight and thickness. This done, sit the pot on the worksurface, set out your brown slip and black iron oxide, and take time to consider just how you want the pot to be decorated. Do you want a traditional incised design grid with a stylized animal motif? Or would you prefer say an uncluttered smooth surface with just a single incised and slipped neck-band? See our working drawings etc.

When you are ready to start decorating, set out the overall design with a delicate incised line, as shown. Now mix the brown slip and a pinch or two of black oxide to a smooth, lump-free 'paint', and give the whole pot two generous coats.

When you have finished coiling, consolidate the form with a metal kidney tool and a wooden beater.

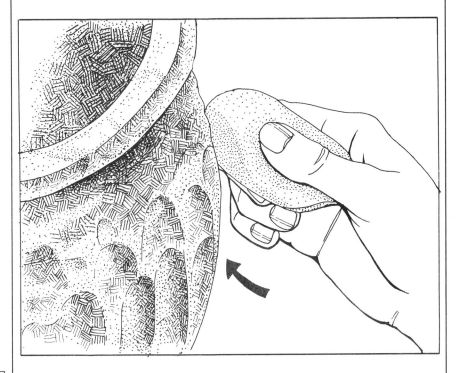

When the slip is dry, that is set and non-tacky, go over the whole pot with the back of a spoon or a bone tool, and take it to a compacted, burnished, high-shine finish. Note — when you have burnished the pot you may feel that the incised decoration needs to be re-established; if this is so, make sure that you don't leave any sharp edges or cut too deep. Finally, when the pot has been slip covered, incised and burnished, then it can be left to slowly dry.

FIRING AND FINISHING

Support the pot in a plastic bowl, or on your lap, and work and shape its interior with a metal kidney scraper.

Place the 'chalky' dry pot upside down in the kiln; no need for stilts or spurs, close the kiln door, leave out the spyhole bung, and then turn on the power. Aim to slowly take the temperature up, say 0–600°C over an eight or nine hour period. When the temperature has reached 600°C, peep through the spyhole to check that all is well; then turn up the heat and set the controls to cut out at about 850–870°C. Finally when the pot is fired and just cool enough to handle, daub it with butter and polish it to a high-shine gunmetal finish.

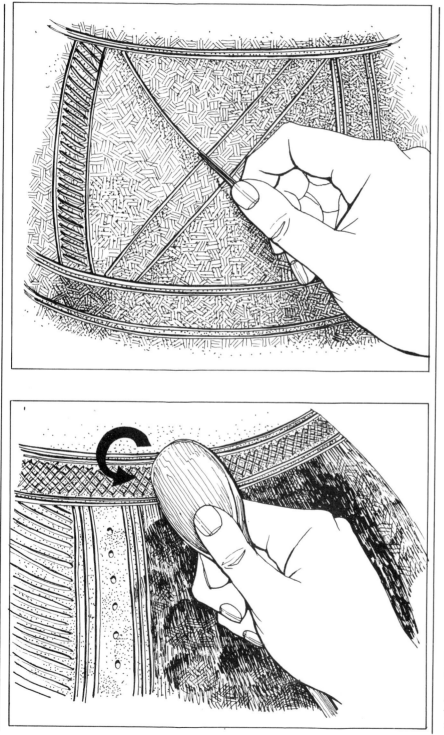

Set out the incised lines of the designs and motifs with a stick-tool — don't cut too deep.

When the designs have been incised and the whole pot slip covered, wait until the clay is leather-hard and then burnish it with the back of a spoon — work with a firm tapping, 'round and round' action.

Finally, make a cane and raffia base quoit.

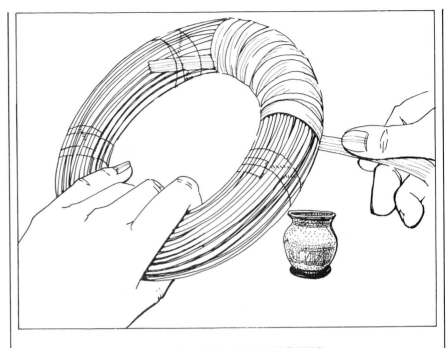

HINTS, TIPS AND NOTES

Clay coils can be round in section, flat, long, short, and so on, no matter; the real secret of coiling and hand-building is keeping the clay moving, and controlling the total form and the speed of drying.

When you are working on the dome-base, you might have problems closing up the final hole; concentrate on the outside, beating and shaping, then finish the inside when the pot is firm enough to handle. When you turn up the kiln for its final 600–850°C firing, make sure that you close the spyhole. Pots of this character look best burnished, unglazed and fired at around 800°C — if the temperature goes much above 890°C the slips, oxides, ochres and burnished shine 'dull off' and lose their finish.

Pots can be coloured and polished with butter, margarine, black-lead, boot polish, wax furniture polish, even milk and cream; it might be a good idea to make a few test tiles and run some experiments using you own mixtures and recipes. Pots of this type and character need not be black oxided; they can be fired in a gas or wood reduction kiln, (see glossary).

If you want to sit this round-based pot on a flat surface, make a small cane, fibre or raffia quoit.

ENGLISH MEDIEVAL INLAID TILE

METHOD · SLAB MOULDING AND SLIP INLAY

Working drawing design grid — the scale is two grid squares to one inch — the finished tile is 6 inches by 6 inches and 1 inch thick — note the depth of the inlay.

INTRODUCTION

Inlaid floor tiles were being made in England as early as the middle of the Thirteenth century; six inch square, inch thick slabs of red earthenware clay were painstakingly hand pressed with relief carved wooden blocks; the indented designs and motifs were topped-up with white slip, and finally, after a deal of scraping and trimming, the tile was raw-lead glazed and then 'once' fired.

Inspirational — (a) a four-square tile group with white inlay and lead glaze, fourteenth century, could be English, but probably French (b) a fourteenth century floor tile, Winchester (c&d) English medieval tiles from the wall of the apse, Great Malvern Priory Church.

Throughout the Medieval period, itinerant bands of tilers 'set up shop' around grand building projects, churches, cathedrals and royal houses, and made many thousands of such tiles. Of course as these tiles were conceived and designed by simple craftsmen and worked from hand carved wooden blocks, so the motifs tended to be bold, basic copies of earlier wood and stone carvings; geometrical 'four-tile' patterns and fleur-de-lis; coats of arms and heraldic beasts; and just occasionally a 'picture' plaque; that is to say a collection of tiles that fit together to make up a much larger design. This method of tile making waxed and waned over the next three or four hundred years, until by the end of the Eighteenth century it was more or less totally forgotten and considered to be a 'lost art'. Fortunately however in the Nineteenth century, with the romantic craft revival, and the renewal of interest in all things Medieval and Gothic, Minton and Co, the tile manufacturers, set out to rediscover the long lost inlaid tile techniques.

After ten years or so, and a great many trial and error experiments, Herbert Minton hit upon a wet, 'plastic' inlay process that used plaster moulds, liquid slips, metal frames and laminated clays. Between 1850 and 1890 mass produced 'Encaustic Medieval' inlaid tiles became fashionable and eventually so cheap that they were used to decorate everything from railway stations to small villa back-kitchen sculleries. It has been said that High Victorian design was initiated by tile makers and that tile making was the great art of the nineteenth century.

CONSIDERING THE PROJECT

TECHNIQUES, TOOLS AND MATERIALS

Start this project by searching out examples of Medieval church tiles and high Victorian encaustic tiles, and if possible take a trip to the Gladstone Pottery Museum near Stoke on Trent and see their tile collection. It might also be a good idea to look round demolition sites in some of our inner city areas and see if you can find whole or broken tiles. When you eventually get to see a tile, and better still if you can see a broken tile, notice the depth of the inlay; the thickness of the tile; the beautiful characteristic smooth hard-edge lines of this design, and the flat areas of colour. and, most important of all, note how floor designs are built up from 'four-tile' unit patterns. Finally, when you get to see some tiles, make tracings, rubbings and sketches.

For this project you need a quantity of well sanded, lightly grogged, red earthenware clay, a quantity of 'just for plaster' rough clay, a small amount of white/cream earthenware slip, a quantity of potter's plaster, a grocery carton, plastic sticky tape, a workboard, a quantity of 'honey' or clear glaze, a metal straight edge, a knife, a sponge, a measure, a selection of wire loop-tools, a rolling pin, two 1 inch thick guide sticks, a canvas rolling out cloth, a collection of plastic bowls and jugs, and of course last but not least the use of a small gas or electric kiln.

FIRST STEPS

MAKING THE WORKING MODEL

Once you have had a look at our various working drawings and inspirational material, and seen and touched a tile 'in the real', then you are ready to start. Take your rough 'plaster only' clay, work it until it is relatively free from lumps, bumps and bits of plaster; then arrange your rolling cloth, batterns and tools so that they are all within reach. Bang a lump of clay down on the cloth, and using the 1 inch thick sticks as guides, make a tile that is 6 inch square and at least 1 inch thick. As you work, lift and turn the clay so that it has an even 'grain', aim to make a working model that has a smooth surface, finger rubbed edges, and well set up right-angled corners.

Now take your working drawings, tracings and pencil press, and pin prick transfer the lines of the design to the working face of the clay. This done, have a good look at your designs, then take the wire loop-scoop tools and very

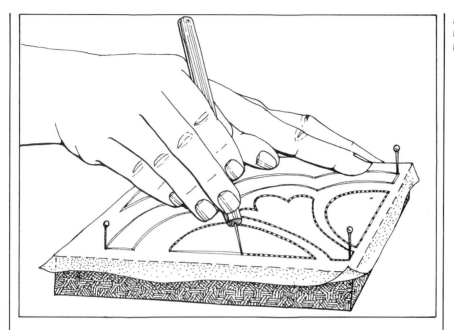

Pin-prick the lines of your design through to the face of the tile working model.

carefully lower the areas that make up the white inlay parts of the design. Try to keep the little hollows clean lined and crisp edged, and work them until they are a little less than ¼ inch deep.

Use wire scoop-tools and lower the parts of the design that are to be inlaid – try and keep the edges crisp and smooth.

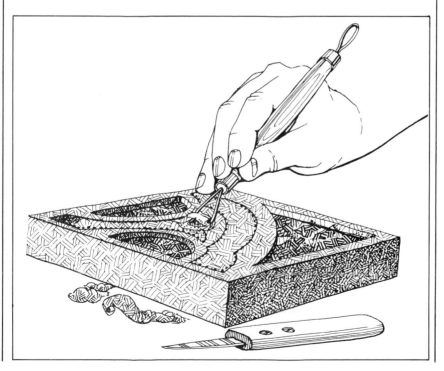

When you are modelling, consider just how the depressions will eventually mark out the lines of the inlay; with this in mind, sharpen up the working model until it is nigh on perfect.

MAKING THE PLASTER MOULD

Take the working model, give it a checking over, and then be ready with the grocery carton card, the workboard, the plastic sticky tape and the various plastic bowls and jugs. Now arrange the working model tile square on the workboard, and build round it a plaster-box that is at least 10 inches square and 2 inches deep; see working details. Place the tile so that it is sitting fair and square in the middle of the cardboard mould — that is, arranged so that it has a 2-inch border between it and the sides of the box. When you are sure that the plaster-box is the correct size, as described, strap it up with sticky tape, and reinforce the outer sides with buttresses of clay,

Build a plaster box round the working model, and support the walls of the box with wads of clay, note — the walls are 2 inches high, and there is a 2 inch wide border round the working model.

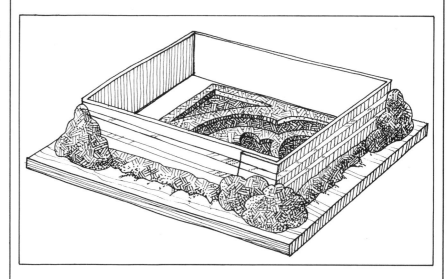

When the box is ready, and you are sure that it is not going to burst at the seams and leak plaster all over your workshop, mix a quantity of plaster, as described by the manufacturer, then pour it over the working model and top-up the plaster box to a depth of at least 2 inches. This done, wait awhile for the plaster to give off heat and set hard, then remove the cardboard box, turn the slab over, and very carefully dig out the no longer needed, working model. Finally, take a knife and trim and bevel the outer edges of the slab and the inner edges of the tile-former, as illustrated.

ROLLING AND PRESSING THE TILE

Wipe down the worksurface making sure that it is absolutely free from plaster, then place the plaster slab and arrange all the tools and materials. Start by banging down a ball of well wedged and kneaded clay, and rolling a slab that is, all round, a little larger than the 1 inch deep 6 × 6 inch former.

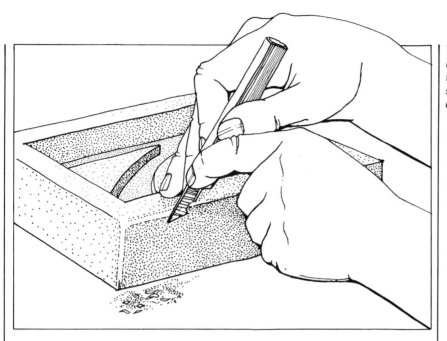

When the plaster has set, remove the boxing and the now unwanted working model, and trim and bevel the plaster — see how the hollows of the tile now appear as raised areas.

This done, take the slab of clay, flop it down into the plaster mould, then, with rolling pin, hands and sponge, force it down into the former. So you work, rolling the slab of clay into the mould, and then with thumbs and a sponge, easing the clay into-and-over all the little sharp angles and corners. Note — if you need to add a little more clay to bulk out the back of the tile, smear and roll the added clay, making sure that you don't trap pockets of air.

To start, roll out a 6 inch by 6 inch by 1 inch thick slab of clay.

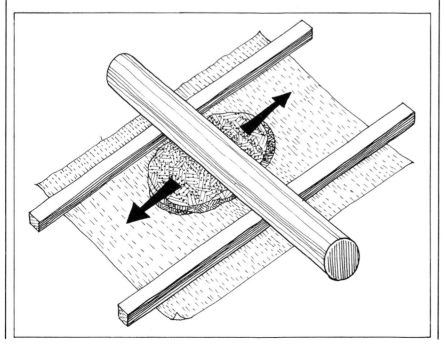

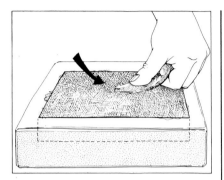

Once you have cleaned up the mould, roll out a 1 inch thick slab of clay and force it into the former — use a rolling pin and your thumbs to force the clay into all the angles and corners.

When the moulded tile has shrunk away from the plaster, put it on a workboard and fill up all the little hollows with thick creamy white slip.

Finally, leave the tile until it has dried and shrunk slightly, then, using a workboard as a support, flip the mould-clay-board sandwich over, and remove the mould. You should now have a beautiful crisp edged tile all ready to inlay.

WORKING THE INLAY

While the red ground clay is still sticky and damp to the touch, take a jug of prepared, thick as you can get it, white earthenware slip, and top-up the little pools of the design. Now wait awhile, and then add more slip until the white areas of the design are more bumps than hollows. Finally, when the whole red ground, cream slip tile has dried off to leather hard, take the metal scraper and metal straight-edge, and shave down the inlaid decoration.

Remove the clay little by little, and aim to cut away the slip overflow, and to reveal and establish the characteristic hard lines of the inlaid motif.

Lastly, rub and burnish the tile until it is smooth to the touch, then put the finished tile on a clean and dry board.

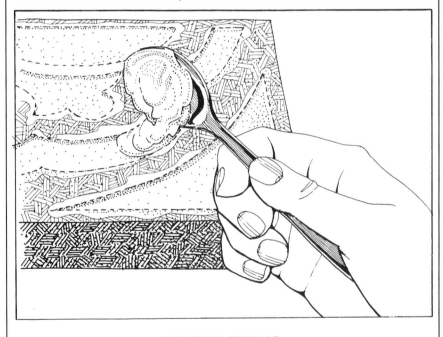

BISCUIT FIRING

When you are working on a project of this character, that is making a number of identical moulded items, try and set out your working area so that you can be making several pieces at the same time. So for example you could have one tile in the mould, another being topped up with slip, and yet another waiting to be finished — a sort of mini production line. When you are drying the tiles, keep an eye on them, and if they look to be curled up at the edges, or warping, turn them over and of course check that they are not in direct sunlight or draughts.

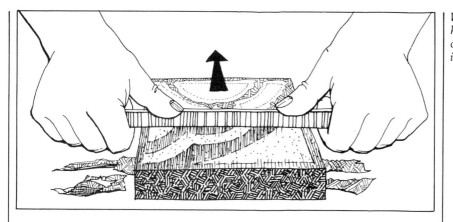

When the white slip has set to a leather-hard, take a metal straight edge, scrape off the surface of the tile and reveal the inlaid design.

When the tiles are completely dry, they can be biscuit fired. Place them face-up on the kiln shelves, open the spyhole bungs, close the door, and turn on the power. Take the kiln temperature up very slowly, say 0–600°C overnight, then set the cut-out for about 900°C.

GLAZING AND FIRING

When the tiles have been biscuit fired, look them over and reject those that are warped and cracked; then be ready with the bucket of prepared honey glaze and the sponge. Take a tile, hold it face down between thumb and

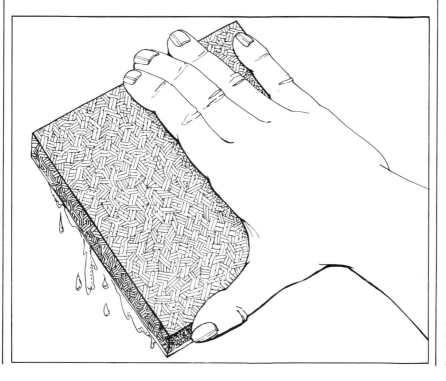

Finally, when the tile has been dried and biscuit fired, glaze the inlaid surface with a clear or honey earthenware glaze.

outstretched fingers, as illustrated, then gently lower it about $^1/_8$inch into the glaze. Now slowly lift the tile clear, let it drain for a second or two, then put it carefully to one side. And so you work each tile, wiping off glaze blobs as you go, and generally making sure that they are evenly glazed.

Finally, place the tiles face-up in a glaze kiln, switch on the power, and set the firing to the glaze manufacturers recommended temperature, as described in previous sections.

HINTS, TIPS AND NOTES

When you are buying your clay, look through the catalogues and search around for a well sanded, finely grogged red earthenware clay — if in doubt, make contact with local potters and suppliers and see if they can recommend a suitable clay.

When you are considering a motif, study your working drawings and inspirational material, and see how the hollows of the design need to be worked within the tile area. See also how the white inlay is clear of the tile edge.

If you find, at the drying stage, that the tiles are badly warping, try another clay body, or maybe slow down the drying.

When you are preparing the white/cream slip, pour off all the free water and try to get a mixture that is very thick, non runny — just like blancmange.

CHINESE TRAY

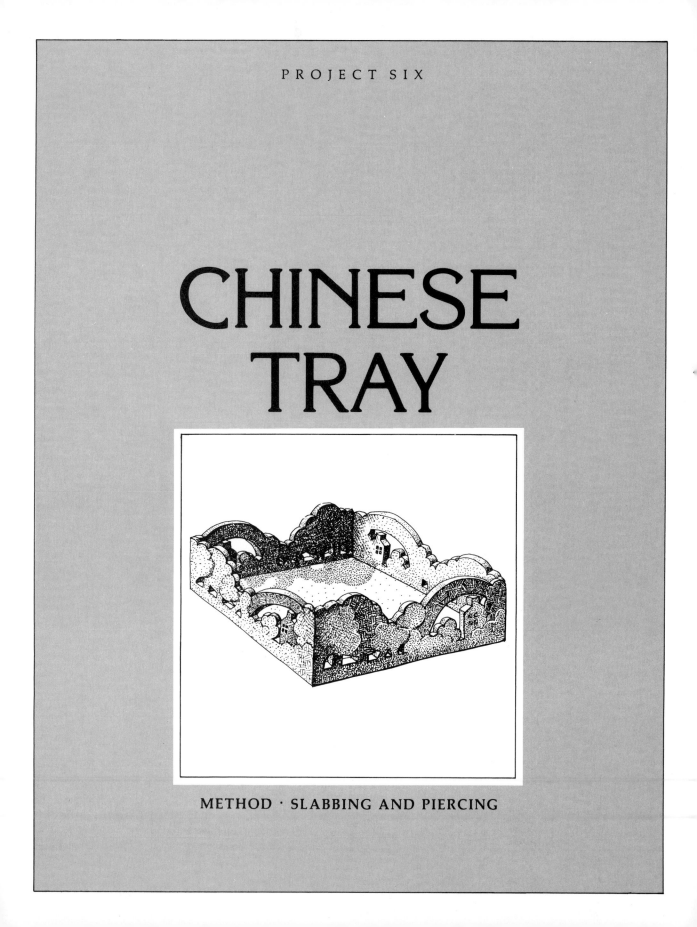

METHOD · SLABBING AND PIERCING

Working drawing design grid — the scale of the upper grid is four squares to one inch, and the scale of the lower plan, views and section is one square to one inch.

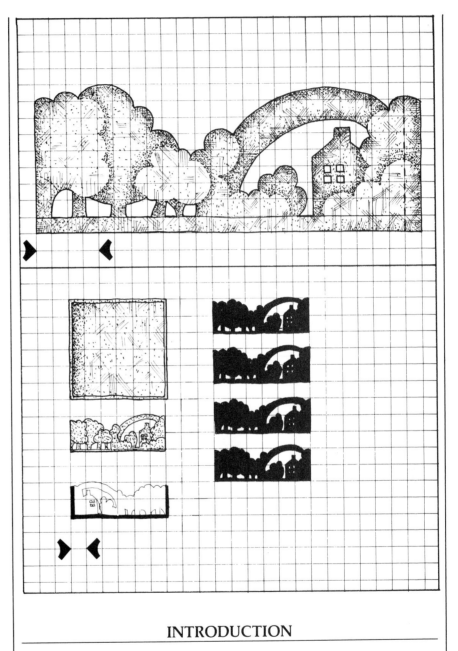

INTRODUCTION

The Chinese have a pottery making tradition that goes back at least four thousand years; massive boldly painted earthenware funerary jars; hard white, deeply carved flasks; delicate bowls made of porcelain; cups, flagons, figures, beakers and bottles; all conceived and made with an elusive vital dynamism that has inspired potters the world over. But best of all, and in many ways the most characteristic, are the beautifully built and delicately

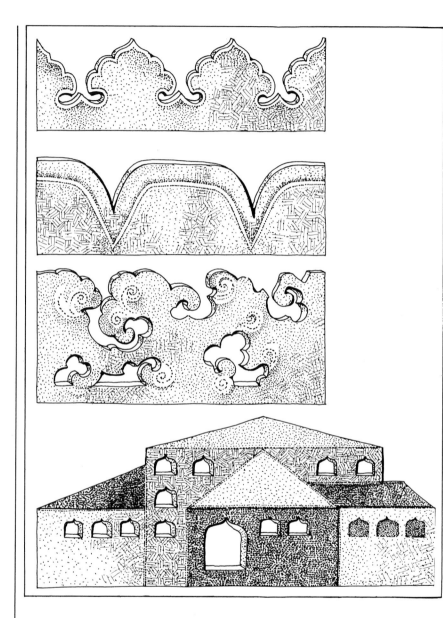

Inspirational – Traditional Chinese, and Chinese inspired, cut and pierced motifs.

worked, slabbed and pierced wares. Little trays with cut and fretted sides; minute model houses complete with windows, doors and roof tiles; colourfully painted 'tomb' groups with cut and pierced chariots; octagonal Cheng Te flower pots; food boxes; Tea Ceremony trays; foliated porcelain bowls, and so we could go on. From a very early date, Chinese pottery was so 'ahead of the field', that it influenced potters in Korea, Indo China, Japan, and eventually the whole Western world.

So, if 'slabbing' for you is a boring secondary school pottery building technique of making untold numbers of characterless ashtray type dishes, then think again and take a fresh look. Slabbed clay can be curved, rolled, moulded, pinched, feathered, pierced, fretted and snipped into all manner of exciting shapes. If you have a flare for graphic forms and want to work in a manner that has been described as 'modern' and 'geometrically exciting', then look to slabbed and pierced ware; many potters consider it to be, at one and the same time, the most traditional, the most up to date, and the most unshackled of all the building techniques.

CONSIDERING THE PROJECT

TECHNIQUES, TOOLS AND MATERIALS

Before you start this project and put hands to clay, of course go and have a look round museums and see Chinese, Korean and Japanese ceramics, but also visit a few big city galleries and craft centres, and note how many of the so called 'new ceramics' have borrowed shapes and forms from, and been inspired by, ancient Chinese slab-built and pierced wares. See also how slab-built pots and forms have been sprayed, pierced, screen printed and decorated in all manner of ways. Finally, take a sketch book and make as many detailed working drawings as possible. Also, while you are in these galleries, collect, beg and borrow illustrated catalogues and suppliers' handouts; they often contain useful inspirational material.

For this project you need a quantity of lightly grogged stoneware clay, a 'clear' stoneware glaze and such tools and equipment as a workboard, a stick-and-wire clay cutter, as illustrated, a measure, a set square, a clay knife, a fine wire piercing tool, various stick tools, sponges, plastic buckets and bowls, pencils and workout paper, and of course the use of a gas or electric kiln.

When you come to use the stick and wire cutter, set the wire on the bottom notch, hold the wire taut, cut the slab, and then move the mass of clay to a new position before you cut the next slab.

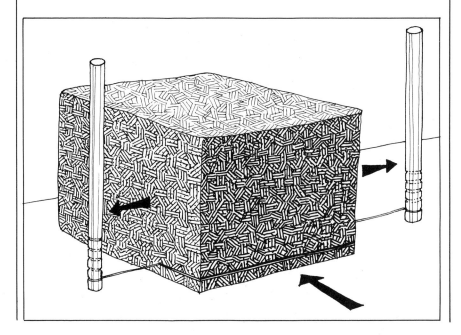

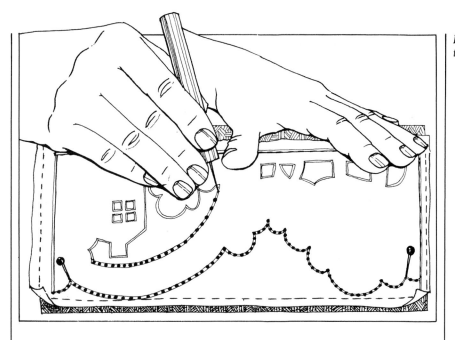

Pin-prick transfer the lines of the design through to the clay slab.

PREPARING THE CLAY AND CUTTING THE SLABS

Take your clay and wedge and knead it as already fully described in previous sections; that is you work it until it is even in texture and completely free from pockets of trapped air. This done, have a long look at the working drawings and details, and see how the little tray has been worked out of a single 6 × 6 inch slab tile, and four 6 × 2 inch sides. Note also how the slabs are all about ¼ inch thick.

When the clay has been well worked, bang it into a block that measures about 8 × 8 × 8 inches, then taking the stick-and-wire cutter, as illustrated, set it on the bottom notch and slice off the bottom slab of clay. And so you continue, holding the sticks apart so that the wire stays taut, then pushing the wire through the mass of clay. As you slice off a slab, move the block to a new position, and eventually place all the slabs on a board to dry out.

You will see, as you drag the wire through the grogged clay, that the slices become grained, grog-dragged and textured — this is as it should be.

CUTTING, FRETTING AND PIERCING THE TRAY SIDES

When the cut slabbed clay is stiff enough to be stood on edge and take its own weight without bending, you can start to cut out the basic shapes. Take your sketched and traced master design and pin-prick transfer the lines of the design through to the clay slabs.

You should now have five ¼ inch thick slabs in all, one cut at 6 × 6 inches and the other four at 6 × 2 inches. Take the 'side' slabs, one at a time, stand them on edge, and using the fine wire cutter, as illustrated, fret the clay making sure that you follow the pin-pricked guide lines. And so you work the clay, slab by slab, carefully cutting out the tree, house and rainbow profiles.

Support the side slabs with clay buttresses, then use a taut wire to cut the profiles.

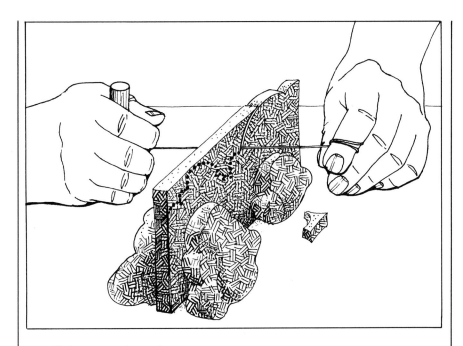

Try all the time to keep the cutting wire at 90° to the working face of the clay, and aim to cut edges that are crisp, precise and square.

PIERCING THE CLAY

With the 'side' profiles still on edge, and supported with small buttresses of clay, carefully push the fine wire through the clay thickness, and then, holding the wire taut, slowly work round the 'windows' of the design. That is to say you cut away the little areas between the 'trees', and the larger areas in and around the 'rainbow' and 'cottage'. Work with a steady hand and a keen eye, and try to keep the cut lines smooth and even. If, as you are cutting, your wire strikes a piece of grog, either pick it out with a pricker tool, or cut round it and make repairs and design adjustments at a later stage.

Finally, when you have worked all the profiles and piercings, take a damp sponge and very carefully wipe off all the ragged edges. Don't make the edges round and weak, but rather remove the burrs and sharpnesses.

PUTTING TOGETHER

Place the workboard square on the surface and then set out your cut slabs and tools. First position the 6 × 6 inch slab base, then mark out and place the sides. Build on the base, scratch the 'join' areas and paint them with slip, then ease all the slabs into position. Finally, when you have trimmed edges and ends, take little worms of soft clay, and with fingers, stick-tools and a sponge, press and work them into all the interior side and base angles.

Of course you will, as likely as not, come across all sorts of problems: mistakes with measurements, bits breaking off, and the like; so be ready to

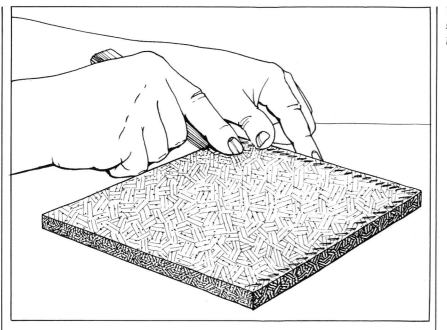

When you have cut the slab base, scratch and slip the joints-to-be, then put it under a plastic sheet.

adjust your designs to fit. Finally, when you have smoothed up all the little corners, angles and edges, very carefully place the pot on a batt and put it to dry in an even temperatured room.

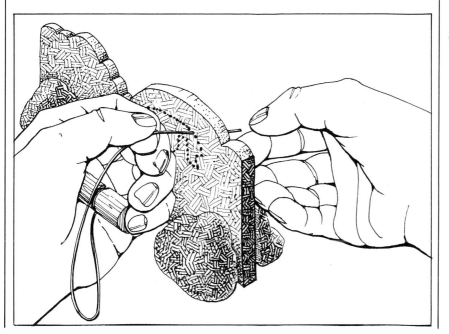

When you come to pierce the design, push the wire through the clay, hold it taut, then follow the design.

Place the tray sides on the slab base, then, using a little slip and thin coils of clay, weld the angle and corner joints.

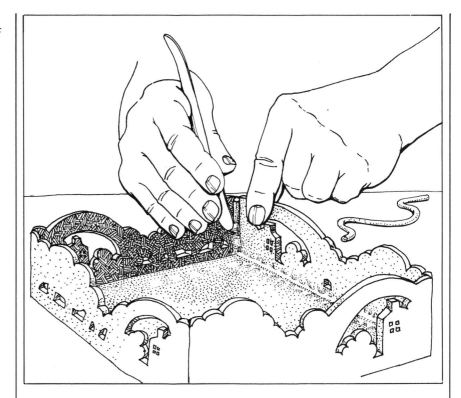

BISCUIT FIRING

When you consider the pot to be completely dry, give it a checking over; just to make sure that it hasn't cracked or got a damp spot; then pack it into a biscuit kiln. Take the temperature up slowly overnight to 600°C, then set the kiln to cut-out at around 1050°C. It is best to switch the kiln on 'low' in the early evening, say about 6 o'clock, let it reach 120°C in the early dawn hours and then get up and re-set the controls so that the kiln reaches 600°C by breakfast time. This slow temperature curve might sound a bit tedious, but it is critical that during a biscuit firing, the pots are allowed to 'steam' or 'smoke' and give off water at the pre 120°C stage.

GLAZING AND GLAZE FIRING

When your pot has been fired to a lowish stoneware biscuit temperature of say 1050–1080°C, it can be glazed and re-fired. Take your bucket of prepared 'clear' stoneware glaze, add water to thin down the mixture, then, holding your pot in outstretched fingers, thrust it in and out of the glaze. This done, take a wet sponge and wipe the base and the lower part of the sides of the pot, making sure that you remove all the glaze. Finally, put the pot in a stoneware kiln, checking of course that all the kiln shelves are sound and there is plenty of clearance for shrinkage and movement, then take the kiln temperature up, as recommended by the glaze manufacturer — 1200–1250°C or thereabouts.

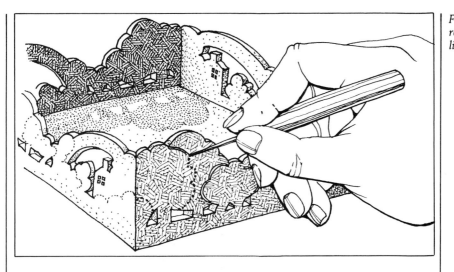

Finally, when the tray is complete, go round the design picking out the incised lines and generally making good.

HINTS, TIPS AND NOTES

We have chosen to work this project in grogged stoneware, but of course you could use a white or red earthenware body, and a coloured 'art' glaze, and fire at a lower temperature.

Slab built pots tend to be extra fragile at the dry pre-biscuit stage, so handle your pot with care, and never pick it up single handed; either cradle it in both hands, or support it on a batt. When you are putting the pot together, note the 'trees, rainbow, house', 'trees, rainbow house', sequence of the sides.

OLD ENGLISH TRAILED SLIPWARE DISH

**METHOD · SLAB PRESSING AND MOULDING
WITH SLIP TRAILED DECORATION**

Working drawing design grid — the scale is two grid squares to one inch — the diameter of the dish is 12 inches and the depth is 1½–2 inches. Note the smooth curves of the rim and the slight upwards tilt.

INTRODUCTION

Huge family sized servers and platters all decorated with trailed and dotted slip; plates, bowls, jugs and tankards covered with slip trailed inscriptions 'Remember God' and 'Of The Earth'; very large 'Toft' commemorative dishes with portraits, dates, names and initials; these are all part of what has come to be known as the 'Old English Slipware Tradition'. Most of us have seen, at some time or other, examples of this ware, maybe in the country museums or actually in farmhouse kitchens, it is characterized by a rich brown

Inspirational – Mermaid motif from a Toft slipware dish dated 1675, also various repeat border patterns. See how it is possible (with the mermaid motif), to build up the design with lines, blocked in areas, and dotted lines.

earthenware clay body, a thick 'honey' glaze, and masses of luscious creamy white and rich red, slip trailed designs, patterns and motifs. Pottery of this character was made as a side-line or 'special' alongside more ordinary every-day plain red and brown 'bread and butter' domestic ware. For a small fee the potters of the seventeenth and eighteenth centuries would make commemorative pieces to order; names and initials, dates of births and weddings, and portraits and emblematic symbols; these were all beautifully worked with flowing, creamy smooth, slips.

The potter would first cover the base clay with slip of another colour, say white slip on a red ground, and then while both were still wet, he would slip trail the designs. The clay slip was contained in little palm held, quill-spouted pottery vessels and then dribbled, dotted and trailed directly onto the prepared ground; no self conscious, overworked, pre-conceived, so called, 'artistic' designs; just a method of working that has been described as free, rhythmic and spontaneous.

CONSIDERING THE PROJECT

TECHNIQUES, TOOLS AND MATERIALS

Before you set out on this project, have a good long look at the working drawings and the step-by-step details, and see how the project involves the use of potters plaster and moulds. Now as you may or may not know, plaster and clay can be used alongside each other, but on no account can they be mixed. If you by chance get chips of plaster in your clay, or spill plaster powder in the slip when the clay is fired, . . . Bang! . . . you finish up with a nasty mess in the kiln and a ruined pot. So before you set out on this project stop awhile and consider: Is your working area big enough for both plaster and clay? Have you got plenty of bowls, buckets and running water? Have you got somewhere to throw away bits of ruined clay and rock-hard plaster? These are all points to consider. Note — you can buy ready-made moulds in a great many shapes and sizes; it might be a good idea to browse through a supplier's catalogue and see what is on offer.

For this project you need a quantity of prepared red earthenware clay, a quantity of rough clay that can be used to make the mould and later put to one side specially for plaster work, a quantity of red, cream and black/brown slip, a quantity of 'honey' earthenware glaze, a rolling pin, two ½ inch thick guide sticks, a cutting wire, a whirler turn-table, a couple of sponges, a soft rubber kidney tool, a scrap of wash-leather, a quantity of potters plaster, a workboard, a rolling out cloth, and such general items as card, scissors, compass, jugs and bowls, and of course the use of a gas or electric kiln.

When you have gathered together all your materials and studied our

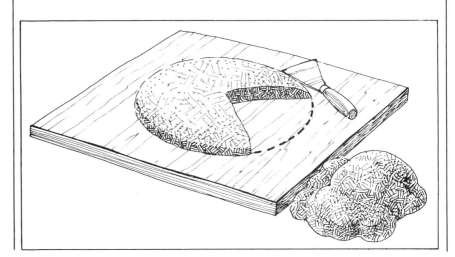

Build up a 12 inch diameter hump of clay.

Using a wood, card or metal template, and various clay cutting tools, make a master mould former that is 12 inches wide and 1½–2 inches high.

working and inspirational drawings, then go along to a museum and have a look at examples of English seventeenth and eighteenth century slipware. If possible search out some of the large, 20 inch diameter 'Thomas Toft' dishes, made in Staffordshire and named and dated 1675. See how these dishes have vigorous design themes, lattice borders and how the patterns, motifs and colours are beautifully worked, balanced and considered. Take note of how the motifs are usually red on a cream ground, edged and lined in with dark brown, and in turn decorated with dots and dashes of cream slip.

FIRST STEPS

MAKING THE MOULD

Decide just how large you want your dish to be, its diameter and depth, then clear the worksurface and arrange your tools and the rough clay so that they are at hand. Start by setting out your workboard with 12 inch diameter circle, as illustrated, and building up a low clay mound. When you have worked a hump of clay that is roughly circular and about 2–3 inches in total height, put it on the whirler turn-table, board and all, and slowly hand turn and tool the clay until it begins to take on the characteristic plate or dish form. Note — the hump of clay needs to be in size and shape the same size as the underside of your dish to be. And so you continue working and turning the clay lump until it is just the right shape, and nicely tooled and finished. This done, take the stiffish card and cut strips that are about one inch wider than the total height of the hump of clay. So for example as our hump of clay is about 1½ inches in height, the strips need to be at least 2½ inches wide. Take the card and, with sticky tape and rough clay, build a wall right round the clay former, as illustrated.

Now for the tricky bit — clear your whole work area and set out the plastic bowls and jugs, plaster, water, stirring sticks and plenty of newspaper. Half fill the bowl with cold water, then gently sift in the plaster, say two pounds of plaster to every pint of water, until the plaster appears as a little peak or island. Now very carefully stir the mixture until it is just a little thinner than single cream. After a few minutes, when the plaster has started to thicken like blancmange, carefully pour it over the hump clay former until you have topped up to the height of the card retaining wall. Note — it is very difficult to say just how much plaster you need, so mix a little extra, and then pour the waste into an old grocery box or into a plastic bag.

Finally, when the plaster has set rock-hard, peel away the card, turn the plaster slab over, dig out the clay, throw away all the odd bits and pieces of plaster, and then clean up the worksurface. It is worth a mention at this stage that there are of course many pitfalls; not mixing enough plaster, plaster going off, card walls bulging and sagging, plaster oozing out, and such like, so keep your wits about you, and be well prepared with cloths, newspaper, old grocery boxes and plenty of water.

PRESS-MOULDING THE DISH

When your plaster mould has been trimmed, cleaned, washed and dried, then it is ready to use. Spread your rolling cloth out on the clean worksurface and have ready the ball of prepared red earthenware clay and all the other tools. Roll out the clay, smoothing and pressing as you go, and aim to make a slab

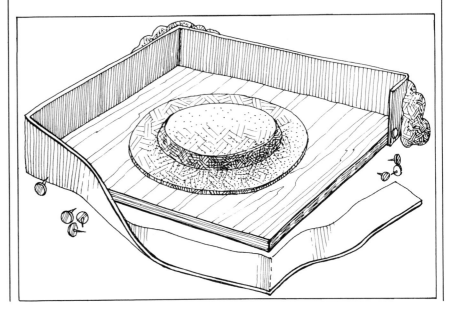

Position the mould former on a workboard and using clay and card, start to build the plaster box. The box, from the board surface to the top of the card, is about 2½ inches. Finally, top-up the box up with plaster.

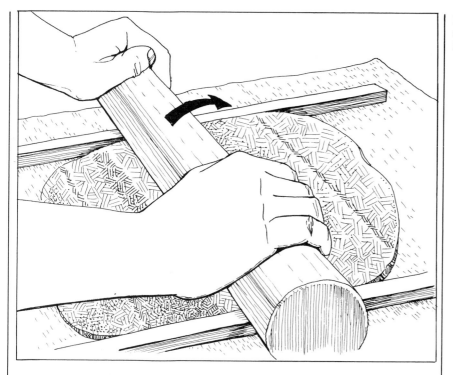

When you have made the plaster mould, roll out an 18 inches wide and half inch thick slab of prepared clay.

that is about 18 inches across and ½ inch thick. When you are sure that your rolled out slab is free from lumps, bumps and air pockets, take up the plaster mould and position it face down on the clay.

Now in a single smooth, controlled 'heave', flip the whole cloth, clay and mould 'sandwich' over on the bench so that the cloth is uppermost. Carefully peel away the cloth and place the mould on the whirler turn-table. This done, dribble a few drops of water onto the clay and then start to smooth and press with the sponge and rubber kidney tool. Work with a gentle smoothing and persuading action, all the time turning the whirler and mould, and gently easing and wiping the clay. Don't try to pull or jab the clay into shape, but rather slowly stretch and work the clay so that it fits and follows the lines of the mould.

Finally take up the cutting wire and with a taut thumb-pressing action trim away the rind of unwanted clay from around the mould, and then with a damp wash-leather, smooth the cut rim until it is nicely rounded in section.

PREPARING THE SLIP AND SLIP TRAILERS

Have a good look at your slip, then pouring off or adding water, as the case may be, stir it until it is free from lumps and bits, and of the consistency of thick cream. Now pour or squeeze-suck the slip into the trailers and then have a few trial workouts on some scrap clay. You should now have three loaded slip trailers in all, red, cream and black/brown, and also a jug of cream slip.

Place the slab of clay in the mould and ease and work it into position with a rubber kidney and a few drops of water or slip.

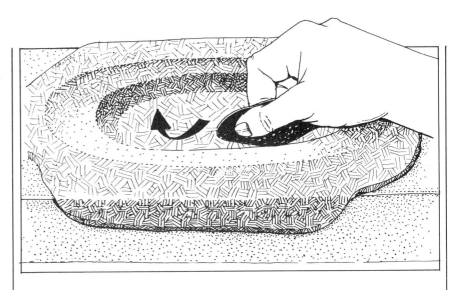

DECORATING THE DISH

Before you start, have a last look at your inspirational material and see how the designs are well organized so as to fill the ground, but at the same time loose, direct and bold in style.

Start by coating the moulded clay dish with creamy white slip ground; that is to say you half fill the red clay mould with slip, slew it round until the base clay is covered, then pour off the excess. You should now have what looks to be a cream coloured dish; wait a few minutes for the shiny slip to dry out and dull off, then start slip trailing. Note — while you are waiting for the ground slip to dry off slightly, it is good practice to clean up the worksurface, loosen

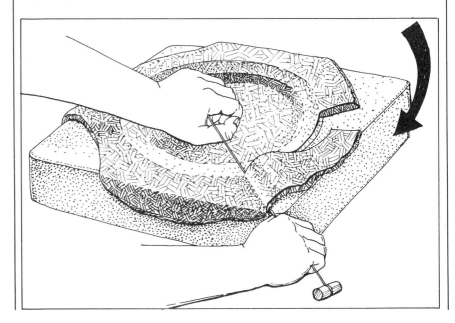

Take a taut cutting wire and cut away the rind of clay from around the dish.

up your wrists by having a trial run with the trailers, and also making sure that there are no dangling plaits, cuffs, ties, ribbons and apron strings.

Start by blocking in the larger areas of the design with the red slip; that is, you draw the slip trailer across the dish, (not quite touching the dish), and at the same time you gently squeeze and trail slip as you go. This done you outline with the black slip, rework some areas with the cream slip, and finally dot the black outline with the white slip.

There are of course many variations on the slip trailing theme; slip lines can be combed and joggled; slip can be dobbed in little pools; blobs of slip can be shaken and marbled; you can use red on white on red, and so on. If you make a mess, no problem; you just sponge out the whole dish, let it dry, slightly and then have another go. Note — if different slip colours are trailed one on top of another, no matter, as long as they are a smooth creamy consistency the colours will stay hard edged and not run.

Finally, when you have achieved a satisfactory design, put the dish to one side and let it slowly dry out.

TRIMMING, FETTLING AND BISCUIT FIRING

When the dish is leather-hard and able to support its own weight and the slip is well set, take it out of the mould, knife-trim or fettle the sharp underside lip edge and sponge off all the bits and burrs. When the dish is completely dry

Pour a little prepared slip into the moulded clay, slew it round so as to cover the clay, then pour off the excess.

Use a loaded slip trailer, and very carefully work your design — note, when you are slip trailing don't actually touch the dish with the slip trailer — keep it just clear.

and nicely fettled, pack it into a biscuit kiln, leave the spyhole bung open, and set the controls at 'low'. Aim to take the temperature up very slowly, say 0-600°C overnight. Finally, keeping the temperature rise smooth and constant, especially at the 120°C stage, slowly raise the temperature and set the kiln to cut-out at about 900°C.

GLAZING

Take your lead-free honey glaze, mixed with water and as described by the manufacturer, then set out the biscuit fired dish and the various bowls, buckets, jugs, water and sponges. Dust off your dish with a soft brush, and then swiftly fill it with liquid glaze. Tilt it so that the inside surface is covered, and then in a single smooth, 'up, over and around' action pour off the surplus glaze so that the dish rim is covered. Fortunately with slipware dishes of this size and character, only the inside surface is glazed, so finally just wipe off the underside of the rim with a damp sponge and the job is done.

GLAZE FIRING

Take your glazed dish and with great care, pack it into a glaze kiln making sure that it is well clear of the sides of the kiln and neighbouring pots. When you are sure that all is correct, set the kiln at 'low' for a couple of hours, just so that the glaze can give off 'free' water, then set the kiln to cut-out at about 950–1020°C.

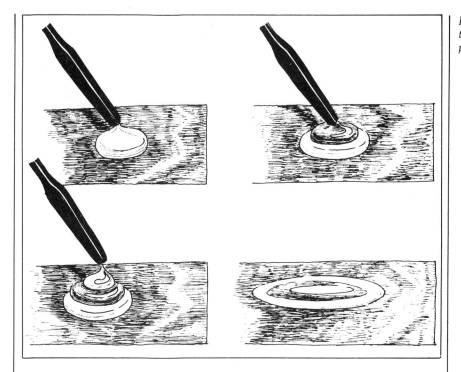

Finally, there are any number of slip techniques, for example slip can be pooled and then allowed to settle.

HINTS, TIPS AND NOTES

When you are working with plaster, never pour waste down the sink or into a drain, but rather pour it into a 'throwaway' box, let it set and then give it to the dustman.

When you are wiping and easing the slab of clay into the mould, only use a few drops of water, or better still, use a few drops of slip.

If you find that there are air pockets in the rolled or slabbed clay, spike them with the pricker tool. If, when you are using the slip trailers, the slip flow falters or stops completely, stop and check that the nozzle isn't blocked with a lump of slip.

When you are decorating the dish, be careful that you don't jolt or jerk the mould.

When you are placing the glazed dish in the kiln, make sure that kiln dust or fragments don't drop onto its surface. If you make a blunder at the glazing stage, don't poke or dabble around with a brush, but rather wash off the glaze, let the dish dry, and start again. With a large flattish dish of this character, don't use spurs — they might result in the dish warping.

NEW ENGLAND 'KEEPING ROOM' DISH

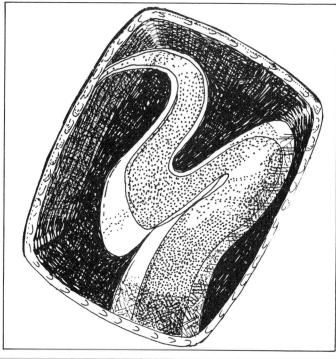

METHOD · SLIP MARBLING AND SLAB MOULDING
WITH PULLED FOOT ADDITIONS

Working drawing design grid — the scale is two grid squares to one inch — the dish is 12 inches in diameter and about 3 inches in total height — note the three feet and the pie-crust rim.

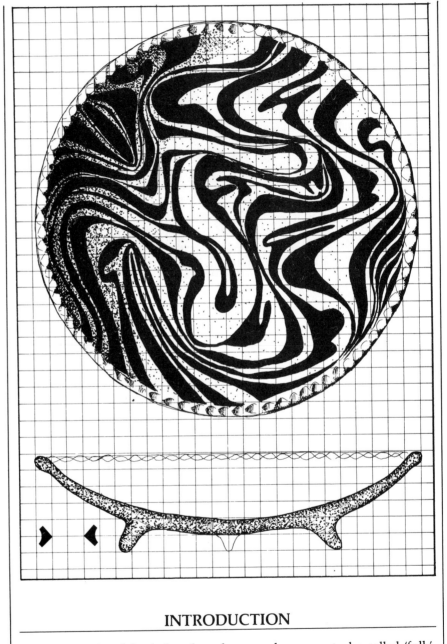

INTRODUCTION

Slip decorated and lead glazed earthenware has come to be called 'folk', 'peasant' or 'keeping room' pottery, because up until the seventeenth and eighteenth centuries it was used primarily in rural farmhouse kitchen situations. Huge English bowls and dishes decorated with wonderfully free slip-trailed designs and motifs; beautifully worked 'green' glaze slipware from Hungary; massive flower and bird decorated plates; platters and

Inspirational – using the marbling technique, it is possible to make a variety of traditional patterns – slip can be random marbled, given a quick jerk to achieve a bold and dramatic design, or carefully placed with a trail and then allowed to flow and follow the contours of a dish or mould.

pitchers from Poland, and so we could go on, describing slipware from all over pre-nineteenth century Europe.

It is thought that the slipware tradition started in the Near East and gradually spread over the Old World, Spain, Italy, Germany, France and England. And of course it didn't stop there; when the American colonies were being established in the seventeenth century, so the European settlers tended to look to their mother country when they were setting up 'just like back home' communities. Each colony introduced its own particular type of slipware pottery; the Pennsylvanian Germans took their 'Tulip charger' dishes, all decorated with trailed slip; the Dutch had their Sgraffito ware, and of course the New England colonialists had their marbled and feathered pottery. Initially the pioneers actually took their pottery with them, so it would have been English, Dutch or whatever, or they imported it from their mother countries, e.g. large quantities of slipware were made in Bideford, North Devon, and sent to New England; but later, of course, the new Americans made their own pottery and only looked to the Old World for design inspiration.

For us, slip marbled, slab moulded and footed dishes characterise all that is best of what has come to be called, 'New England' slipware. The techniques are basic and true to the 'old ways'; the forms are honest and noble, and, most important of all, the designs echo all the strengths of traditional peasant wares.

CONSIDERING THE PROJECT

TECHNIQUES, TOOLS AND MATERIALS

At the outset of this project, try and visit as many rural museums as possible and get to see examples of combed, marbled and feathered slipware. English, American, European, it makes no matter as long as the pottery relates to the 'tied to the earth' folk and peasant traditions of wood fired, slip decorated, lead glazed earthenware. When you get to see examples of this type of

Inspirational – you can, if you so wish, go for a mixture of slip techniques, and maybe even include a trailed and feathered design.

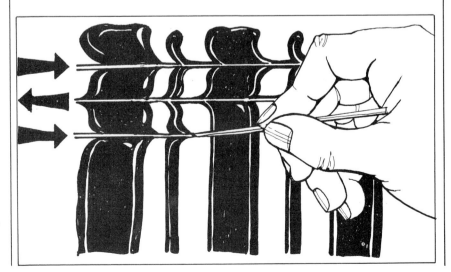

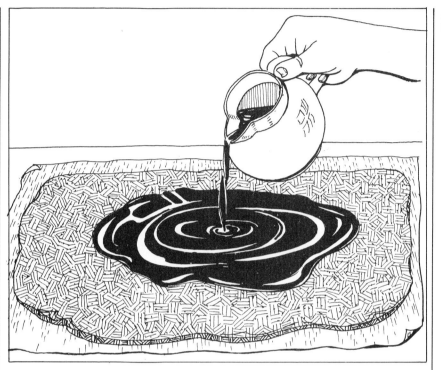

Roll out a slab of clay (on a cloth on a board), then pour out the prepared slip.

pottery, note the simple and direct treatment of handles, lips, lugs, feet and 'pie-crust' edges, and see also how the bowls and dishes are only glazed and decorated on the inside. Finally, when you feel that you understand how the wares were put together and decorated, them make as many detailed and inspirational sketches and notes as possible.

As for tools and materials, you need a quantity of red earthenware; look for a well sanded character clay, prepared red and cream slips, a workboard and rolling out cloth, a rolling pin and two guide sticks, (½ inch thick), a 12 inch diameter plaster hump or mushroom mould, a cutting wire and stick tools, a small quantity of 'honey' glaze, the use of an electric or gas fired kiln, and such general workshop items as, sponges, a rubber kidney, whirler turntable, pricker tool, pencils and workout paper, and a variety of plastic jugs and bowls.

PREPARING AND ROLLING THE CLAY

Take your wedged and kneaded red earthenware clay and set out all the tools and equipment so that they are within reach. Now smooth out your rolling cloth, making sure that it is free from bits of dry clay, then bang down your working clay, arrange the two guide sticks and then set-to with the rolling pin. Work and roll the clay as if you were rolling out pastry; that is, you roll a little, ease the clay up from the cloth, roll some more, and so on, until the clay is nicely worked, free from air pockets and generally of a shape and size to suit your particular hump mould.

When you have achieved a slab of clay that is about 15 inches across and ½ in thick, slide it on its cloth onto the workboard, then clear the worksurface and be ready with the slips.

MARBLING THE CLAY

Take your red and cream prepared slips, making sure that they are free from lumps and of the consistency of thick smooth-flowing cream, and decant them into two small jugs. This done, take the red slip, pour a pool onto the middle of your rolled out clay, then lift up the workboard and gently tilt and move it so that the slip covers all. When the clay is completely slip covered, take both the cream and red slips and pour them alternately one on top of another.

You should now have, as it were, a largish 'bulls-eye' pool of two-colour slip, say cream on red on cream on red, as illustrated. Note how the two slips spread out on each other, but stay as separate colours. Now once again take up the workboard and gently tilt and move it so that the pool of slip runs and moves over the clay.

With a marbled decorative technique of this character, each and every design will, of course, be different; this will make the items that bit special, but with some trial and error and a deal of experimentation you will be able to predict and control overall design themes. For example, if you only give the slips a quick swish, then the design will be bold; or if you keep the board moving and turning the design will be fine grained; and then again you can direct the initial slip flows with trailers and cut-paper stencils, and so on. It is possible to achieve any number of completely personalized designs — see the inspirational illustrations.

MOULDING THE DISH

When your slipped and marbled slab of clay has dried out to a dull flat finish and is just short of being soft-leather hard, then very carefully place your

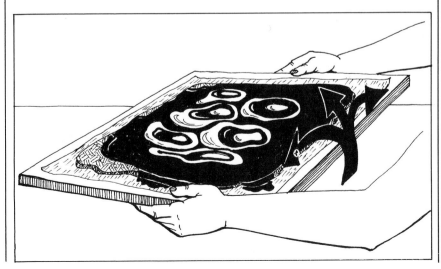

When you have poured out the coloured slips, one on top of the other, then take up the board and gently tilt it so that the slips move and flow.

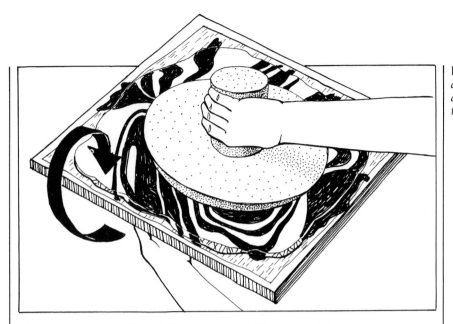

When the slip has dried off and gone dull, place the mushroom mould head down on the slip marbled clay, then take the whole works and flip it over.

plaster hump mould head down in the middle of the slab.

Now for the tricky bit — with both hands, take the workboard, rolling out cloth, clay and all, and with a controlled flip, turn the whole works upside down. This done, remove the board, carefully hand-press and ease the cloth so that the clay slab fits over the mould, then very gently peel away the cloth. You should now have a moulded dish that is smooth formed, cloth textured, and free from creases and wrinkles.

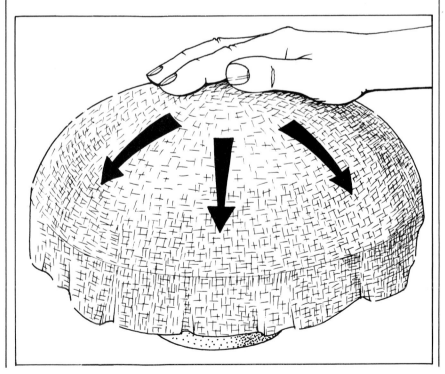

Take away the board, then gently ease the cloth supported clay over the mould.

Take a needle pricker tool and trim off the unwanted rind of clay.

Finally, take a pricker tool, or better still a fine cutting wire, and slowly turn and trim the rind of unwanted clay from the rim of the dish, as illustrated, then with a sponge, smooth and make good the cut edge.

PULLING THE KNOB FEET

When you have trimmed and worked the dish, as described, have another look at the working drawings and details, then, by eye or with a compass, establish the triquetra placing of the three knob feet. Now take three small lumps of prepared clay and work and pat them so that they are, in shape and size, like little pears. This done, dab the fat ends of each pear in slip, and then place and push them onto the marked out dish. Now thumb-smear each of the pear shaped lumps of clay, as illustrated, and work them so that they are well jointed onto the dish base.

Finally, using slip lubricated fingers, grasp and stroke out the three knobs so that they appear, horn or bud-like, to be smoothly growing out of the mass of clay that is the dish base.

THE PIE-CRUST EDGE AND FINISHING

When the dish has dried off and started to shrink away from the plaster mould and the three pulled feet are stiff enough to bear the total weight of clay, very carefully place your hand on the dish base, flip the dish and the mould over, and then remove the mould.

Now stop awhile and see how the three foot knobs support the dish, and how the slip marbled surface is smooth and undamaged. Take the wooden

Mark out the position of the three feet, then place the three pear shaped lumps of clay and ease and thumb smear them into the main body of the dish.

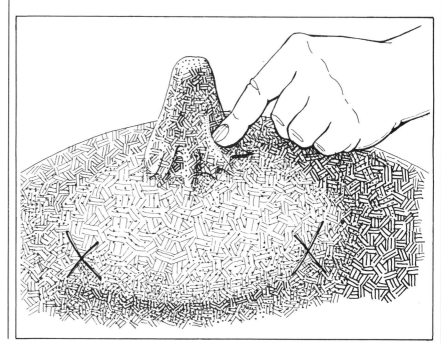

stick tool and go round the dish rim giving it the characteristic pressed pie-crust edge, as illustrated. This done, take a knife and trim and adjust the feet so that the dish sits straight and true. Finally smooth up all the rough edges with a moist sponge and then put the dish to one side to dry out.

DRYING, BISCUIT FIRING, GLAZING AND GLAZE FIRING

When the dish is completely dry, turn it over and check that the rim and feet are sound; then with great care, place it, rim side down, in a biscuit kiln. Take the kiln temperature slowly up past the critical 120°C, and when the contents have 'smoked' and 'steamed' at 120–600°C, set the firing to go up to, and cut out at, 1000°C.

When your dish has been biscuit fired, then it needs to be glazed. Stir and prepare the 'honey' earthenware glaze, as described by the supplier, wipe down the worksurface, decant the glaze into a jug, and dust out the dish. Now carefully half-fill the dish with glaze, then, at one and the same time, tilt-turn-and-angle the dish so that the liquid glaze runs over the marbling, over the pie crust rim and back into the glaze bucket.

This done, turn your dish, base side up, wipe away any glaze splashes and then stand it on its own three feet in a glaze kiln. Finally check that all's well, then set the kiln to fire and cut out as recommended, — say at about 1000–1080°C.

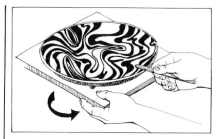

Finally, when you have taken the dish off the mould, take a small stick tool and give the dish rim a pie-crust edge.

HINTS TIPS AND NOTES

Slipware marbling is best managed in flattish, circular, hump moulded dishes; when you are looking to buy or make a plaster mould, go for one that has shallow, smooth, uncomplicated contours.

When you have laid down the initial red slip ground, wait awhile before you go onto the next stage and give the clay a chance to dry out.

When you have marbled the clay slab, let the slip dull off to a dry hard matt before you attempt the not so easy, flipping over of the clay onto the mould — you should be able to touch the slipped surface without leaving a mark.

With rolled, slabbed and moulded dishes of this character, the base of the dish is left biscuit and unglazed, the only decoration is the pressed pattern left by the rolling out cloth. Use a cloth that has a loose weave, say a bit of sacking or hessian.

We use a stick-tool to make the pie-crust rim, but traditionally, potters made and used a little roller tool, rather like a pastry roller.

If, when you remove the hump mould, the slipped surface of the dish is wrinkled, it means that the mould is too domed, and consequently the dish too deep — go for a flatter mushroom-like form.

ART
DECO
VASE

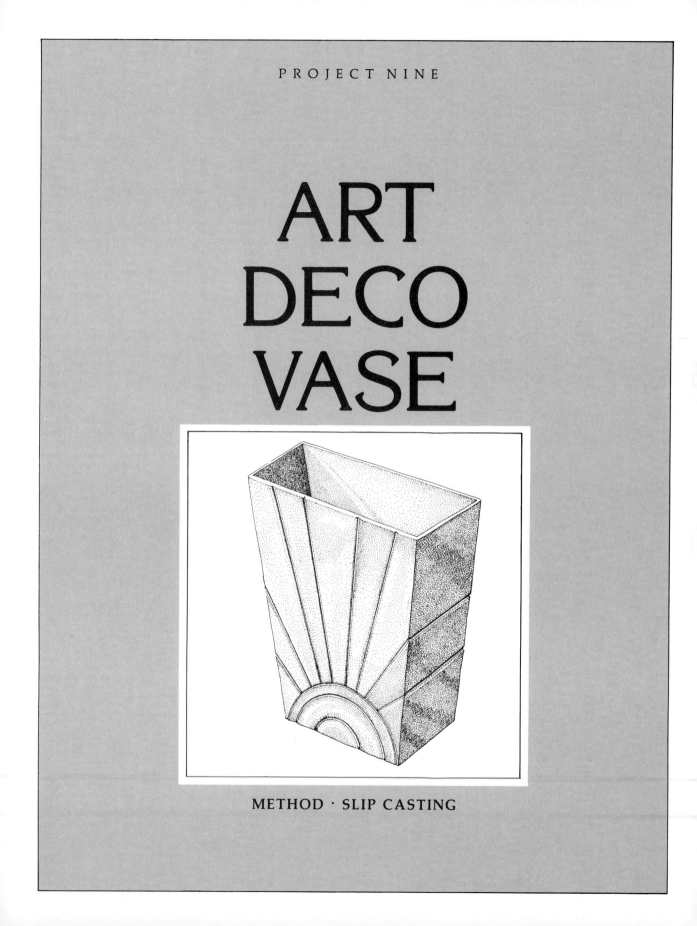

METHOD · SLIP CASTING

Working drawing design grid – the scale is two grid squares to one inch – note the total height of 7½ inches, and the flared rim.

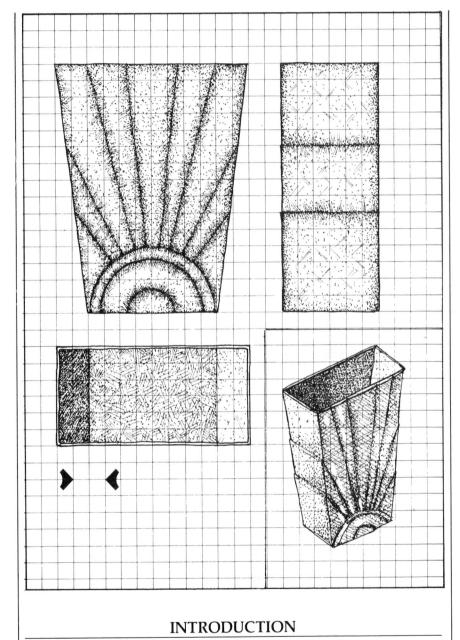

INTRODUCTION

Although the term Art Deco is now used loosely to describe just about all the arts, crafts and industrial forms that were produced between the wars, say 1920–1938, it originally meant belonging to, or inspired by, the great Paris Exhibition of 1925 — 'l'Exposition Internationale des Arts Decoratifs et Modernes'. The idealistic artists and designers of the period set out to produce only 'modern functional forms that are expressions of production',

Inspirational – a selection of possible Art Deco motifs.

but of course they couldn't help but be influenced by the times in which they lived. So on the one hand Art Deco forms were created that followed through the initial concepts of only using modern materials and techniques, chrome chairs, Bakerlite plastic electrical fittings, and the like, and on the other hand the Art Deco concept gave expression to products overlaid with popular imagery — Egyptian masks on furniture, Cubist motifs on textiles, Aztec stepped architectural forms, and of course 'sunbursts' on just about everything.

Pottery forms of the Art Deco period are characterized by being angular and round cornered, precision cast, and slickly surface decorated with all manner of sharp-edged, geometrical, painted and applied motifs; sunbursts, zig-zags, scalloped clouds and stepped triangles.

CONSIDERING THE PROJECT

TECHNIQUES, TOOLS AND MATERIALS

Before you set out on this project, have a look at the working drawings and step-by-step details and note how the vase has been designed so that it can be cast in a simple one-piece mould. See how the vase is wider at the rim than at the base, so as to allow for maximum air flow during the slip drying stage, and how it has been worked so that it can slide freely out of the plaster mould.

We can have chosen to work a classic Art Deco form with a stepped profile and a rather obvious sunburst design; but of course there is no reason why

Start by making a full size working model, and mark out the patterns and motifs with a shallow 'creased' incised line.

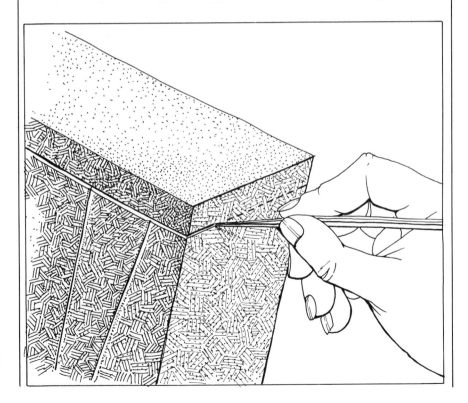

your vase shouldn't relate to some other period or form, and be say tall and round sectioned and decorated with flowered motifs or whatever.

For this project you need a quantity of white earthenware casting slip — best if you buy it ready made-up, a pound or two of rough clay to be used only for plaster work, a quantity of potters plaster, some transparent earthenware glaze, a grocery carton of a size and shape to take your vase, a metal whirler turn-table, a ruler and callipers, a couple of wooden batts, some stick tools, a sponge and rubber kidney, a selection of plastic bowls and jugs, the use of an electric kiln, and of course such other workshop items as card, scissors, sticky tape, pencils and workout paper.

FIRST STEPS

DESIGNING AND MAKING THE WORKING MODEL

Before you put hands to clay, take a pencil, paper and ruler, experiment with a variety of heights and profiles, and draw out a whole batch of possible vase forms. However bear in mind along the way, that as the vase is to be slip cast in a one-piece mould, it needs to be slightly flare-mouthed and free from undercut projections and hooked additions.

When you have a clear picture in your mind's eye of just how your vase is to be, draw it out to full size and finalize the various dimensions and decorative characteristics. Now pin your working drawings up so that they are within view, wipe down your working area, and arrange all your tools and materials so that they are at hand.

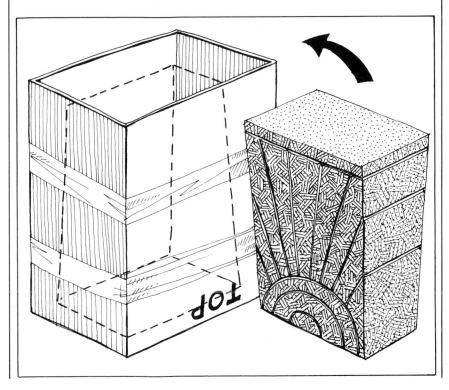

When you have made a working model and you are sure that all is correct, place it bottom up in a cardboard plaster box, and top the box up with plaster.

This done, take the rough clay, workboards, measure and callipers and knock-up a full size solid clay, working model of your vase-to-be. Don't hollow out the clay block, but do aim to give it a really high finish, paying particular attention to the total form and the decorative motif. If you look at our working drawings you will see that although the sunburst design fits the form and is a major element, it is in fact no more than a smooth shallow-worked fold or dip; no sharp cuts, incisions or stuck on additions, just a subtle V-section crease that follows the lines of the design.

Once you have blocked out the model and have achieved a form that is smooth, flare-mouthed and symmetrical, and have checked that the rim and base are parallel, then you can think about making the plaster mould. Note — if you look at our detailed drawings you will see that we have given the working model a 'collar' at the rim — this is trimmed off the cast vase at the leather-hard stage.

MAKING THE PLASTER MOULD

Clear your worksurface of all good clay, then have at the ready the working model, the plaster, the grocery carton and all the various jugs, bowls, buckets and tools. Start by making sure that the grocery carton is going to take your working model with at least one inch all-round clearance. For example, as our vase is 6 × 3 inches at the rim and about 7½ inches high, we need a box

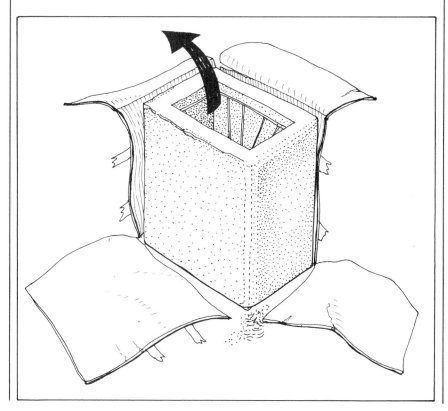

When the plaster is dry, carefully remove the clay working model and pull off the cardboard plaster box.

about 8 × 5 inches at the rim and 9 inches high. Now check the box over, fill any holes with clay, and for extra strength strap it up with bands of string or sticky tape. This done, carefully position the working model, rim side down, in the carton, and set it on a level worksurface.

Now half fill your plastic bowl with cold water and gently sift in the plaster until it peaks above the water, (use about two pounds of plaster to every pint of water). Stir the mixture until it is free from lumps and powder, leave it be for a couple of minutes, then pour it over your working model and top-up the mould box.

When the plaster is good and hard, tear away the cardboard box, turn the mould over and very carefully dig out the clay working model. Finally wash the mould under cold running water, trim and bevel the sharp outside corners and put it to one side to dry out.

SLIP CASTING THE VASE

When the plaster mould is completely clean and dry, then you can make a cast. Take the casting slip, mixed, stirred, and carefully prepared, as described by the manufacturer, and when all is ready, fill the plaster mould right up to the brim. Now wait a few minutes for the slip level to sink, then keep topping the mould up. After about 10 to 15 minutes, tilt the mould slightly so that you can estimate the thickness of the slip build-up at the rim, (¼ inch of build-up will dry to a finished thickness of about ⅛ inch), then empty the slip back into the bucket. Now leave the mould upside down to drain, then put it right-side-up to dry out.

Finally, after about two to three hours, when the slip build-up within the mould has dulled off and started to shrink, the mould can be turned up-side-down and the cast carefully removed.

Fill the plaster mould with casting slip, tilt the mould and check on the slip build-up.

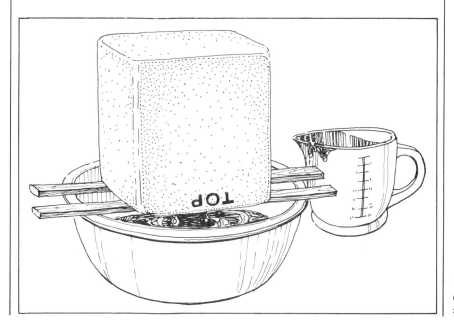

When the build-up within the mould is about a quarter inch thick, pour off the slip and let the mould drain and dry.

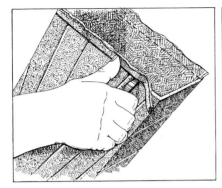

When the cast has dried and shrunk away from the plaster mould, it can be removed and carefully fettled and trimmed.

FETTLING OR TRIMMING THE CAST

When the cast vase had dried out to a leather hardness, it can be carefully handled and worked. Take a sharp clay-knife, or better still a scalpel, and trim off the spare 'collar' of clay at the rim of the vase. Try to achieve a smooth, round-sectioned, level rim, adjusting and making good as you go. This done, rub and wipe the cut rim with a piece of damp wash-leather, and put the vase to one side to dry out.

BISCUIT FIRING

When the pot is totally dry, that is powdery and 'chalky' to the touch, then it needs to be biscuit fired. Handle the now fragile vase with caution, and put it in a biscuit kiln. Set the kiln at low, leave the spyhole bung open, then aim to raise the temperature from 0–600°C overnight. Finally, set the kiln to full power and switch the cut-out to come into operation at around 1000°C.

GLAZING

Take your bucket of clear earthenware glaze and your biscuit fired pot, and set up the working area with plastic bowls, jugs, glaze-sticks, the whirler turn-table and a sponge. First half-fill the vase with glaze, slew it around and pour off so that the whole interior of the pot is glaze covered.

This done, set the vase, rim-side-down, on a couple of bowl-bridging glaze sticks and in turn put the bowl on the turn-table. Now very slowly turn the whirler and, at one and the same time, pour the thin glaze over the vase, Aim to cover the whole vase, bottom, sides, rim and all, with a thin even coat. Finally when the glaze is dry, take the sponge and water, and remove most of the glaze from the vase base.

GLAZE FIRING

Take your glaze covered vase and, supporting it on at least three spurs, place it very carefully in a glaze kiln. Finally check that the vase is well clear of other pots and the sides of the kiln, then set the kiln to fire to the glaze manufacturer's recommended temperature. Aim to take the temperature up very slowly for a couple of hours, just so that the glaze can dry out, then, checking that all is well, close the spyhole, turn up the heat, and complete the firing.

HINTS, TIPS AND NOTES

Casting slips can be made up from basic ingredients or purchased ready mixed — look through a supplier's catalogue and see what is on offer.

With a project of this type — that is slip casting in a one-piece mould, it is vital that the vase be slightly wider at the rim that at the base; bear this in mind when working on initial design sketches.

If you intend building the working model over an extended period, cover it with plastic film so as to keep the clay workable.

When you have finished pouring plaster etc, wash the various bowls as quickly as possible, and make sure that you pour the waste into 'throwaway' containers. The first cast from a new mould is usually less than perfect and considered to be a 'waster' — use it for firing and glaze trials.

Try to keep the vase cast unfingered and free from finger and tool marks.

Finally, when the cast has been biscuit fired, it can be glazed inside and out.

VICTORIAN DOLL'S HEAD

METHOD · SLIP CASTING

Working drawing design grid — four grid squares to one inch — the head measures about 3½ inches from the top of the head to the tip of the chin, and 3 inches from ear to ear. Note that this head is open at the neck, rather than at the top of the head, and note also the pierced 'dress' holes.

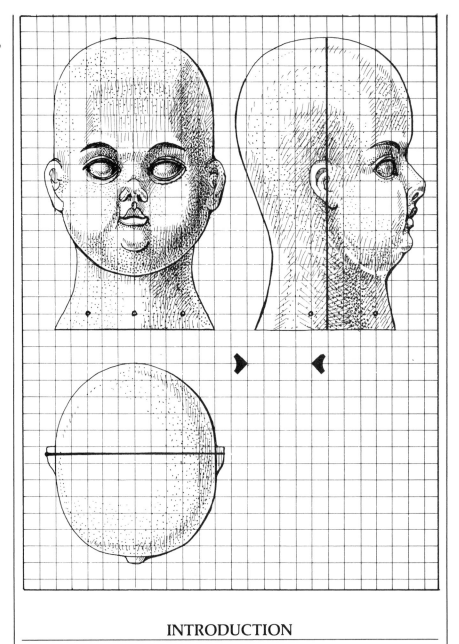

INTRODUCTION

Throughout the ages dolls have been made, the world over, from just about every material that you can think of. Curious plant fibre dolls from tribal Africa; printed, sewn and stuffed rag dolls in Edwardian Europe; carved and jointed wooden dolls in colonial America; wax dolls in eighteenth and nineteenth century France, but the best of all are the 'Victorian' porcelain dolls that were made in Europe from about 1860. Hollow-cast and beautifully

Inspirational – (a) a modern reproduction 'Jumeau' doll (b) A nineteenth century doll made by the famous French Jumeau family (c) A modern reproduction French doll.

worked, dolls of this type can be seen in many of our museum collections; large smooth pink-faced beauties, with red cupid lips, huge innocent eyes, flowing hair, arched brows and all dressed in 'Sunday Best' costumes. Originally dolls of this character were considered to be children's toys, but of course with the passing of time, they have become much sought after and collectable.

For the potter however, cast-slip, doll designing and making, is a challenging activity that can be worked and managed in a relatively small studio with a portable kiln, and a few inexpensive tools and materials. If you are looking for a gentle lead into what has come to be called, 'Hobby Ceramics' or 'Slip cast Ceramics', and you consider small to be beautiful, then this could well be the project for you.

CONSIDERING THE PROJECT

TECHNIQUES, TOOLS AND MATERIALS

Start this project by having a long look at the inspirational illustrations and working details, then go and see a museum collection of porcelain or bisque-head dolls. Ask the museum keeper if you can handle the dolls, then have a close-up look and see how they have been made, worked and put together. See how the head and neck are hollow cast in one piece, and note how some dolls have painted eyes, while others have fixed glass eyes, or even eyes, lids and lashes that move. Finally, make a series of detailed sketched studies of doll features; see if you can capture the essential characteristics, the wide

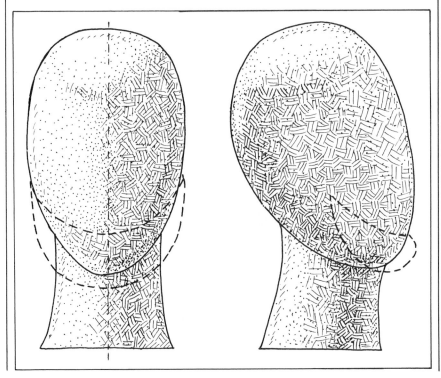

Start to build out the working model — try and get the tilt of the head just right.

eyes, the smooth curved and arched brows, the fullness of the cheeks, and the pert downward turn of the mouth. We have chosen to work a dolls head with painted eyes, but this project can be worked and adjusted as you think fit.

For this project you need a small amount of smooth white earthenware clay, a quantity of fine-grade potter's plaster, a quantity of prepared good quality pre-mixed porcelain casting slip, and of course such modelling tools and items as a whirler turn-table, a timer, a measure, brushes, soft soap, calipers, stick modelling tools, a knife, a cutting wire, work boards, and a selection of plastic bowls, buckets and jugs.

DESIGNING AND MAKING THE WORKING MODEL

Clear the worksurface of clutter, arrange the turn-table so that it is stable, set out your tools and materials, then pin up your working drawings, details and sketches so that they are within view.

Now take your modelling clay and start to build up the basic head, neck and shoulder form; that is, you roll out a ball for the skull, then build out the chin, the nose, and the overall set and shape of the head. Don't be in a rush to start modelling the 'fleshed' features, but rather try to establish the important underlying large shapes and structures.

This done, slowly turn the whirler and consider the model from all angles. Is the tilt of the head correct? Could the head be more rounded and built-out back and front? Are the forms symmetrical? and so on — be critical and spend time getting it all just right.

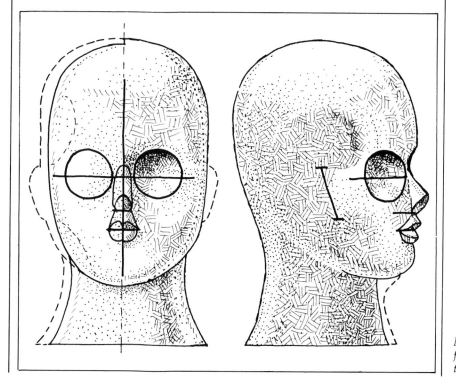

Mark out the position of the various features, and build and model up from the basic form.

Use a measure and callipers and model the features — make sure that the features are symmetrical.

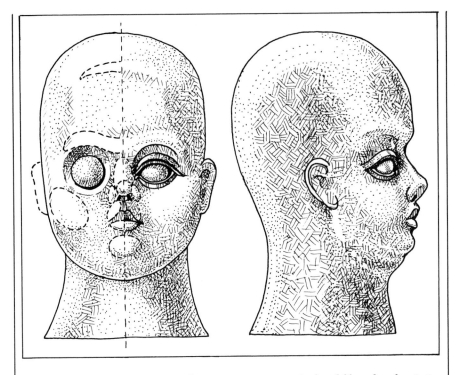

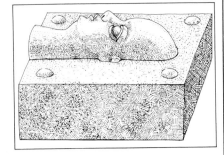

Place the finished working model face up on a workboard and build up a bed of clay — the clay bed should have a smooth surface and finish at the ear level. Note — when you place the location nobs, fix them with slip.

When you feel that the foundation structure is as it should be, then begin to build out the details. First mark out the position of the nose, ears, eyes and mouth — see our working drawings, and note how the eyes are placed about halfway down the face, and how the ears line up with the eyes and mouth. Now place the eye-balls within the hollow eye sockets, and start to model and build out the full puffed roundness of the upper eye lids, and the rather proud arching of the brows. And so you continue, adding the slightly pursed lips, building out the 'snubbed' nose, filling out the cheeks, and generally trying to achieve the overall characteristic rather vacant, slightly jowled Victorian doll image.

As you work, stop from time to time, take the calipers and measure, and check with your working drawings. You should be aiming to make a dolls head that is about 3½ inches from the top of the head to the tip of the chin, about 3 inches from the back of the head to the tip of the nose, and about 3 inches from ear to ear.

Remember as you are working that all the features need to be well rounded; avoid deep undercuts behind and over the ears, and don't make the nose too full. Finally, model and finish the head so that it is absolutely smooth and free from flaws and tool marks.

MAKING THE PLASTER MOULD

When you have achieved a well worked model of the doll's head and it has dried to the leather-hard stage, lay it face-up on the workboard. Now, using thumb-sized pieces of clay, support and build up the head until it is embedded

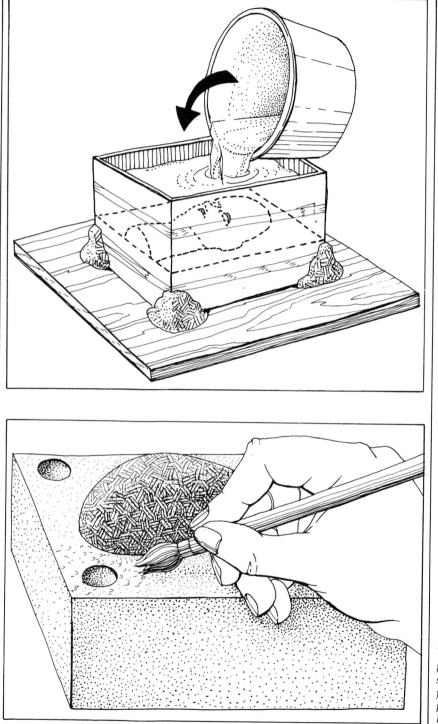

When you have worked the clay bed up to ear level, build up a cardboard plaster box, and top it up with plaster.

When the plaster is dry, remove the plaster box and brush the bed with soft soap. Now with the working model still face down in the plaster, repeat the plaster box building, and cast the other half of the mould.

When both halves of the mould are dry, remove the clay working model and clean up the edges of the plaster.

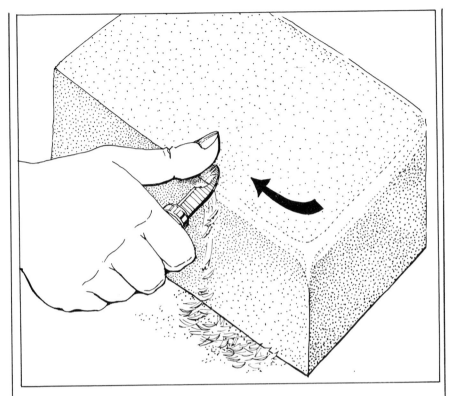

in clay up to the ear-line, as illustrated. This done, smooth and tool the flat bed of clay, and work it so that the front of the head is completely surrounded.

When you have smoothed the bed, take two little marble-sized balls of clay, cut them in half, and then place and fix the half-balls on the smooth clay. Now square-up the sides of the clay bed, and box it in with carton card and clay.

Now for the tricky bit: mix up a small quantity of plaster, as described in a previous chapter, and gently pour it over the boxed-in face. When the plaster is set, turn the workboard over, and carefully dig away the clay bed and plaster-box, until you are only left with the working model and the plaster cast.

You should now have a dolls head embedded face-down in a block of plaster. See the working details, and note how the little half-balls of clay have left four location hollows or cast keys, and how the neck-line of the working model comes flush with the side of the plaster half-mould. Now take the soft soap and give the plaster several brushed on coats. This done, box up the half-mould with card and clay, and top it up with plaster as before.

When the plaster is totally dry and hard, remove the boxing, ease the two halves of the mould apart, and remove the now unwanted clay working model. Now take a soft-hair brush, and very carefully wash the mould under running water until you have removed all traces of clay and plaster crumbs.

Finally take a knife and chamfer and bevel the outer edges of the mould, as shown — this prevents corner chipping and establishes a well defined mould joint.

CASTING THE DOLL'S HEAD WITH PORCELAIN SLIP

When the mould is completely dry, dust it out with a soft brush, label it front and back, and then arrange your tools and materials on and around the work surface. Now dampen the inside of the mould, and strap it up with rubber bands. This done, prepare the slip, as described by the manufacturer; this usually means stirring and letting the air bubbles rise off; then decant it into a plastic pouring jug.

The next stage must not be rushed or in any way hesitant, so be ready with the timer, and make sure that you are going to be undisturbed. Note — the speed of slip pouring must be constant — if you stop for a moment the cast will be rippled and flawed. Place the mould, neck end uppermost, and then top it with the prepared slip — work with controlled swiftness. Now time the slip-setting, and when the slip build-up is as required, say ¼ inch to ⅜ inch depending on doll size and slip type, pour the slip back into the jug and then leave the mould upside down to drain. After about one and a half hours,

Strap up the mould and top it up with porcelain casting slip.

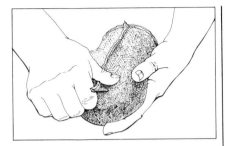

Finally remove the cast from the mould, trim and fettle the joint mark, dry, biscuit fire, glaze and decorate.

when the slip has set and can be handled, trim off the waste from around the neck of the mould, and place the mould face-up on the worksurface.

Now with great care, ease off the top half of the mould, and lift it straight up and away. Have a test to see if the slip is firm, then turn the cast head out of the bottom half of the mould. Finally, trim and fettle the seam and the neck edge with a knife; smooth the fettle marks and cut edges with a finger, and pierce the little sew-and-dress holes, as illustrated.

FINISHING AND FIRING

Dolls of this size, type and character can be finished and decorated in a great many ways; our advice is to make contact with a supplier — see what they have to offer, then decorate your doll's head accordingly. That apart, when the head has been slowly dried, then it needs to be biscuit fired. Very very carefully place it upside down in a porcelain shard and support it in a nest of fine, clean 'placing' sand.

Finally, as with all biscuit firings, slowly take the kiln temperature up through recommended curve, and set the kiln to cut-out at the recommended temperature, (say 1220°C for biscuit firing, and then to about 720°C for subsequent firings).

HINTS, TIPS AND NOTES

'Soft soap' is simply chips of hand soap that have been boiled and simmered in water so as to make a slimy mixture; painted on plaster, soft soap leaves a slightly greasy finish that prevents plaster sticking to plaster.

We have chosen to work this project with a white porcelain slip, but there are other slips — white, cream, brown, earthenware, coloured etc — see a current supplier's catalogue.

As with all plaster and clay projects, you must be careful that you don't get fragments of plaster in the clay stock — either use different work areas, or be scrupulously clean and organised. When you are using soft soap, make sure that you don't get it on the working or casting face of the mould.

COUNTRY COTTAGE JUG

METHOD · THROWING AND WORKING AT THE WHEEL

Working drawing design grid — the scale is one grid square to one inch — note the generous handle and the handle thumb-stop.

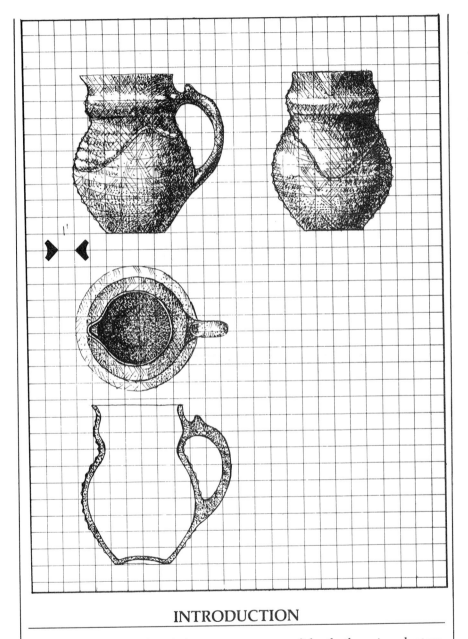

INTRODUCTION

To watch a traditional English country potter confidently throwing planters, pancheons and jugs; to see him raise, shape and form the spinning rich red clay is a most beautiful, stimulating and now unfortunately, a rare craft experience. However there was a time, a hundred or so years ago, when every small cluster of villages had a pottery, and every country cottage kitchen its collection of red and cream earthenware pots.

The 'tied to the earth' rural peasant potter had his supply of locally dug

Inspirational – a selection of country jugs – note the bold shapes, the strong lips and the direct handles.

brick clay, a basic lead-ore glaze, a kick wheel, a few stick-and-bone tools and a raw fuel kiln. One can see in the mind's eye the whole country workshop and pottery-making operation; the potter hunched over his wheel; an apprentice standing by; horses slowly turning pug mills; drying sheds full of half made pots and the roaring wood-fired kiln, marvellous! Of course the eighteenth and nineteenth century village potter had no choice but to use locally found materials and traditional handed down, 'father to son', techniques and forms; but within these tight limits he created all manner of large, bold, honestly made domestic earthenware. Big broad bellied bowls, giant slip decorated platters and plump pouting jugs; these are all part of what has come to be called, the English 'kitchen hearth' or 'country cottage' pottery making tradition.

CONSIDERING THE PROJECT

TOOLS, EQUIPMENT AND MATERIALS

For this project you need a potter's wheel — kick or electric it makes no matter, half a dozen balls of wedged and kneaded, slightly sandy, red earthenware clay, half a dozen carrying batts, two small plastic bowls for water, a sponge on a stick, a cutting wire or cord, a ruler, a needle or pricker tool, a small scrap of washleather, a quantity of earthenware 'honey' glaze, a quantity of cream slip, the use of an electric or gas kiln, and of course such 'around the workshop' items as plastic buckets, bowls and jugs, glaze sticks, brushes, pencils and sketch paper.

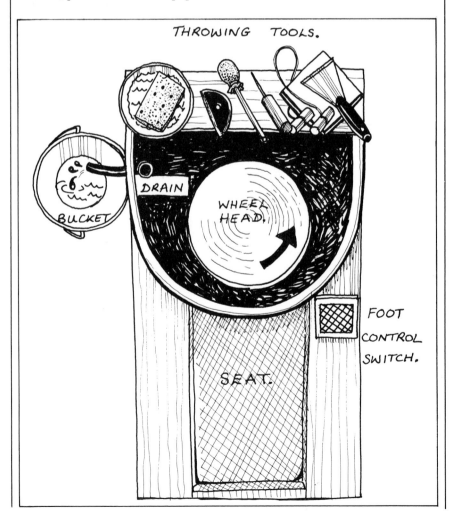

Set your wheel out so that all the tools are comfortably to hand.

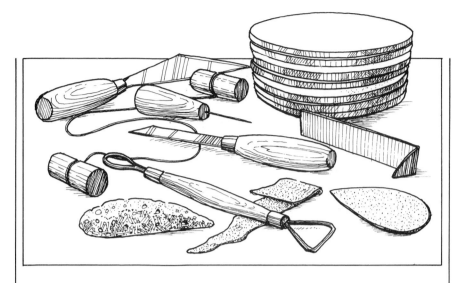

You need a stack of work boards/batts, a turning tool, a cutting wire, a pricker tool, a clay knife, a sponge and one or two shaping tools.

Before you start out on this project, try and handle as many jugs as possible, get to know their qualities, and 'feel' them out for size and pouring. Ask yourself, have these jugs got a good pout to the lip? Do they pour without dribbling? Do the handles fit the size of the jugs? Should some jugs have thumb stops? and so on, until you feel that you understand and appreciate what it takes to make an ideal jug.

Lastly, when you have had a good look at our working drawings and inspirational illustrations, it might also be a good idea to visit a local 'crafts' or 'rural' museum and see if you can study country-made jugs of the seventeenth, eighteenth and early nineteenth centuries. Also, just before you sit down at the wheel, tie back you hair, roll up your cuffs, take off your ring and wristwatch, and generally kit yourself out with old clothes or a coverall apron.

FIRST STEPS

CENTERING THE CLAY

Try out the wheel for size, get to know the controls, then arrange all your tools and materials so that they are to hand, say on the back shelf of the wheel or on a side table.

Now take up one of the balls of prepared clay and, with the dampened wheelhead at rest or spinning, it makes no matter, bang the clay down onto its centre. This done, sprinkle a little water over the spinning clay, have a last glimpse at your inspirational sketches etc, and then to work.

Set the wheel in motion, then tuck your elbows into your waist, brace your shoulders, push your left hand against the side of the clay, cup your right hand over the clay, and finally with a single considered hand-and-shoulder movement, ease the clay into the wheel's centre. And so you continue until you can delicately cup the spinning clay without it juddering or threatening to spin off the wheel.

If you find that your first efforts are a mess-up, and say the clay slides off the wheelhead or gets too water logged, don't despair, but rather clean down the wheelhead with a sponge and start on a fresh ball of clay. Note — with experience, you should be able to centre the clay with a single controlled

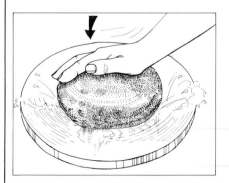

Bang the prepared clay down onto the wheelhead.

With both arms well braced, push the clay into the centre of the spinning wheel.

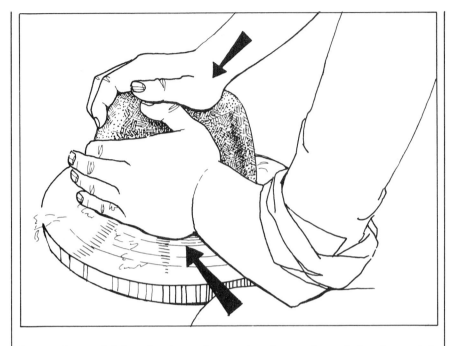

heave of your left hand — keep the weight of your thrust behind your left shoulder and forearm.

WORKING THE CLAY

When the clay is well centred, that is, you can touch it with an almost still finger tip while it is in full spin, dampen your hands, place braced and cupped hands over the centred clay mound, and then in a single easy, 'up-and-in' movement, pull the clay up into a cone shape. This done, steady the cone with linked and cupped hands, and then press it down so that it once again becomes a spinning mound. And so you continue to 'cone up' and 'mound down' until the clay is well placed and of a good even working consistency.

OPENING UP THE CLAY

When the clay has been centred and worked and you can feel its quality and stability, then it needs to be 'opened' out. Grasp your right wrist with your left hand, and then with your elbows braced, thrust your thumb into the centre of the spinning clay mound. Don't let the clay carry your hands off centre — keep your hands steady and firm, and continue the thumb thrusting until you reckon that there is about ½–¾ inch of clay left between your thumb tip and the wheelhead.

This done, brace your wrists, bring your thumbs together, and then with a gentle, smooth 'up-and-in' action, draw the clay up until you have a tall cylindrical form. Now, being extra careful that you don't jar the clay off centre by suddenly whipping away your fingers, 'neck' the cylinder with

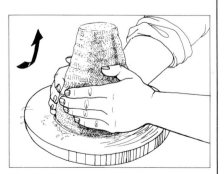

When the clay is centred, cone the mound of clay up and down.

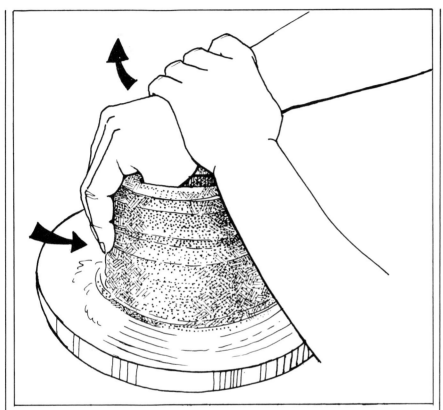

With fingers, thumbs and knuckles, gently apply pressure to the clay and draw up the walls of the cylinder.

Brace your right wrist with your left hand and open up the mound of clay with your thumb.

thumb knuckles and finger tips, as illustrated, and stroke the clay with a firm 'up-and-off' movement. Finally, moisten your hands and wrists, back and front, get your left hand well down into the spinning clay, and then with braced arms and fist-clenched knuckles, bring the cylinder of clay up, as illustrated.

FORMING THE 'BELLY' AND 'NECK' OF THE JUG

When you have opened up the clay and achieved a tall cylinder that in width matches the base of the jug-to-be, then you start to work the various curves and profiles. Have another look at your working drawings, and then with braced arms, enter your left hand into the cylinder and start work.

With the knuckles of your left hand, and the knuckles or finger tips of your right hand working in harmony, exert a little 'squeezing' pressure on the spinning walls of clay. So, if you want the pot to 'belly' out, you increase the outward pressure of the hand inside the cylinder, and if you want the pot to 'neck' in, then you increase the outside pressure. Working in this manner, let your braced hands, knuckles and fingers shape the clay until you have achieved a jug form that has a generous belly and a good upright 'collared' rim or neck.

When you have achieved a pleasing jug shape, trim off the neck with a needle pricker tool.

Finally compress the clay at the rim with a scrap of wet washleather and aim to achieve the characteristic rounded, slightly turned out profile — as illustrated.

PULLING THE LIP

When you consider the pot well shaped, and you have generally checked it over for lumps, bumps and air pockets, then set the wheel in motion and mop out the pot with the sponge-on-a-stick tool.

Now take the point-ended turning tool and trim the pot down at the base until it is nicely bevelled and undercut. This done, dribble a little water onto the wheelhead, and then, with the taut thumb-pressed wire, slice the pot from the wheel. Wipe your hands dry, and then with outstretched and extended fingers, cup or cradle the pot and lift it onto the moistened batt.

So, now for pulling the jug lip; moisten your left thumb and index finger, space them about 1–2 inches apart, place them against the outside neck of the pot rim, and then, with the slip covered fingers of the right hand, work the lip gradually out and over. Don't mess the clay about or try for an overworked 'sulky' lip, but rather go for a lip that is thrusting, bold and firm. Note — when you are stretching the rim, take your time, or you will rip the clay.

PULLING THE HANDLE

Take a largish ball of clay, smack it into a pear shape and then check it over for lumps, bumps and breaks. Now give the fat end of the pear-shaped lump a 'neck', hold it firmly in your left hand as illustrated, wet your hands with slip and then start to work the clay with a smooth downward stroking action. And so you continue stroking and grasping the clay until you have achieved a long tapered 'tongue'. Lastly you run your thumb knuckle down the 'tongue' to give its concave section.

When you consider the handle finished, pinch it off at the fat end and shape

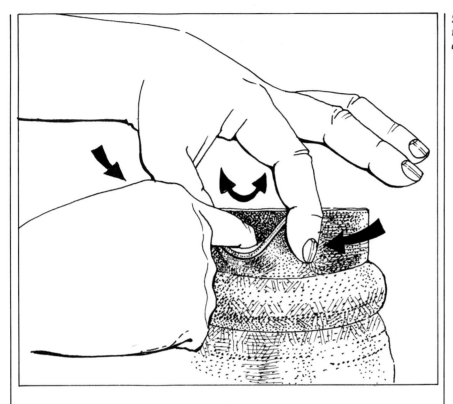

Support the jug rim with your left thumb and index finger, and stroke out a lip with slip lubricated fingers.

it so that it can be butt jointed to the neck of the jug. Finally when the jug has stiffened, bring it and the handle together, as illustrated, and thumb-smear the joint so as to achieve the beautiful direct finish that characterises country ware. This done, stand back and be super critical — does your jug look balanced? Is the lip strong or over pouty and weak? Is the handle of a size to match the weight of the jug? and so on.

SLIP DECORATION

When your jug is dry enough to handle — say just before the leather-hard stage, set it up on the worksurface and have your bucket of cream coloured slip and various plastic bowls and jugs to hand.

Now for the tricky bit — make sure that the slip is well stirred and free from lumps and bits, then take the jug firmly in one hand and lower it, rim side down, into the slip. Aim to cover the whole of the jug rim, the lip, and at least half the handle; be swift, dunk the jug in and out and give it a moment to drain and then set it, right side up, on the worksurface. Finally when you consider your jug finished, put it to one side and dry out.

DRYING AND BISCUIT FIRING

With a large generous jug of this size, weight and character, there is always the chance that the rim or handle will split or break off during drying,

Take a pear shaped lump of prepared clay, and using slip or water as a lubricant, stroke and pull a handle.

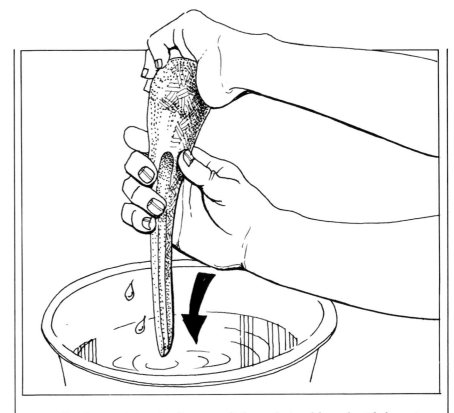

especially if it is sitting in direct sunlight or being blasted with hot air or draughts. Always check the pot at regular intervals, and make sure that it is free on its batt to move and contract. When the jug is totally dry, that is, 'chalky' to the touch, it can be biscuit fired. Set your dry jug inside the kiln alongside other pots, and when you are sure that all the pots are well placed, say biggest and heaviest at the bottom and most delicate at the top, then open the kiln spyhole or bung, shut the door and turn on the power.

With a 'handled' pot of this type it is vital that you don't rush or hurry the biscuit firing; especially during the pre 120°C stage; so aim to take the heat up very very slowly, say 0–600°C over an eight or nine hour period. When the kiln temperature has passed the critical 600°C stage, close the bung, turn up the power and set the kiln to cut-out at around 1000°C.

GLAZING

Take your biscuit fired jug, make sure that it is free from dust and finger marks, and then arrange the bucket of earthenware 'honey' glaze and various sticks and plastic bowls and jugs on the workbench.

Start by taking free water off the glaze, or adding more water, as the case might be, then give it a good stirring. Note — if the glaze is lumpy, then run it through a fine lawn seive. Now decant the prepared glaze into a plastic jug and in turn, pour it into the biscuit fired jug and then in a single swift movement, carefully tilt, tip and turn the jug so that the liquid glaze covers its interior and runs back into the bucket. This done, wait a few minutes for the glaze to dry, then place the jug, rim side down, on a couple of glazing sticks.

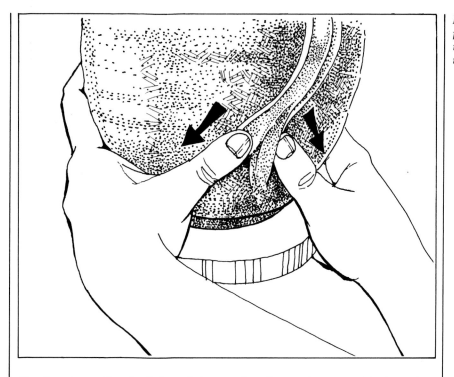

Finally, butt joint the top of the handle, pull it down into a good curve, and then thumb-smear the tail to the underbelly side of the jug.

Finally take up the plastic jug of glaze and walk round your upside down jug, and pour glaze over its sides. Note — with a country pot of this character, leave the base unglazed.

GLAZE FIRING

Take your biscuit fired and glaze covered jug and very carefully set it up in the kiln. This done, check that it is well clear of neighbouring pots and the sides of the kiln, then gently shut the kiln door and turn on the power. Finally set the temperature at 'low' for a couple of hours, just so that the glaze can dry out, then programme the kiln to cut-out at the glaze manufacturer's recommended temperature of around say 1020°C.

HINTS, TIPS AND NOTES

Jugs need to look and 'feel' just right, so spend time making say half a dozen jugs and then pick the best of the bunch.

When you come to the slip decorating stage, make sure that the clay is neither too soft nor too dry — if it is too soft/wet it will collapse and if it is too dry the clay will expand rapidly and also collapse.

When the jug has been 'slipped', it needs to go through a slow controlled drying; it might be a good idea to hold back the drying of the handle and lip by covering them with strips of damp cloth.

Finally, never lift a drying pot up by its handle or rim; always cradle it in both hands and handle with great care.

A GLOSSARY OF TOOLS, TERMS, MATERIALS AND TECHNIQUES

Agate Ware   A type of pottery made of coloured layers of clay. At the preparation stage clays are folded together; this looks a bit like cream and brown marble.

Air Pockets   If air is caught up in clay, it forms an air pocket — such an air pocket expands rapidly in the kiln and shatters pots. Wedging and kneading removes air pockets.

Alumina Sand   Can be used in clay bodies, but it also makes a good bedding or nest when you are firing delicate pots — see Doll's Head project.

Ball Clay   A creamy grey clay that can be fired to a high temperature and is the basis of many earthenware bodies.

Batts   Boards, Tiles or Workboards are all thin tiles, slabs, or discs of clay, wood etc that are used for carrying pots.

Battens   Glaze Sticks or just sticks, are wooden sticks used as slab rolling guides and glazing aids.

Bentonite   Can be added to clays and glazes to make them more plastic.

Biscuit or Bisque   Once fired pottery that hasn't been glazed.

Blisters   Bubbles of gas caused by air pockets or an overfast firing — looks blister-like under glaze.

Blunger   If you reckon on mixing large amounts of slip, glaze or whatever, use an electric blunger — looks like a food mixer.

Body   The clay mix, used to make pots, so you might order say an earthenware body or a stoneware body.

Bone China   A soft white translucent porcellaneous type body or ware — contains lots of bone ash.

Bung   Can either be a pile of shelves in a kiln, or the spyhole stopper. Even though electric kilns often have flaps and slide discs, rather than actual stoppers, they are still sometimes called bungs.

Casting   Slip casting — liquid clay slip is poured into a plaster mould; as the water is taken up by the plaster, so a skin of slip/clay forms; as the slip skin dries, so it shrinks away from the plaster and becomes a caste.

Celadon   A green coloured stoneware and porcelain glaze.

China Clay   A very white Cornish clay used in china, porcelain and earthenware bodies.

Clay   The basis of all pottery bodies — it must be cohesive and withstand firings.

Coiling   A method of handbuilding pots using coils, worms, snakes or slugs of clay.

Collaring   The throwing process of making and turning a pot rim.

Combined Water   Even dry clay contains water; this is termed 'Combined' and is driven off at around 500–600°C.

Combing   A method of decorating with wet slips — slips are stroked and combed with feathers, and the like.

Cones   Small ceramic shapes that melt and collapse at pre-determined temperatures — they are placed inside the kiln as temperature indicators.

Copper Oxide   A metal oxide — gives good greens and reds.

Crackle   A considered decorative glaze fracture or texture.

Crazing   The same as crackle, except that it is unwanted and unintentional.

Dunting   If a pot is fired and then cools too quickly and cracks, then it has 'dunted'.

Earthenware   A low fired pottery ware that is soft, opaque and permeable — most folk, ethnic and country wares are made of earthenware.

Eggshell Glaze   A semi matt glaze texture.

Englobe   Cover slips — that is to say a slip ground — say a white slip over a red body is called an 'englobe'.

Encaustic   Literally meaning to burn in, it is now taken to mean a nineteenth century inlaid tile.

Extrusion   To push soft clay through a metal die — the 'sausage' of clay that is pushed out of a pug mill is an extrusion.

Fat Clay   A good plastic workable clay is described as being fat.

Feather   In slip decoration — meaning to draw the tip of a feather through clay slips so as to make a characteristic feathered design.

Feldspar   Used in clay bodies and glazes.

Fettle   To trim or cut off the seams from a moulded or cast pot.

Fireclays   Clays that can withstand very high temperatures

Firing   To place a pot in a kiln and apply a controlled heat.

Galena   A raw lead glaze, now no longer commonly used.

Glaze   A glassy vitreous coating that covers a pot.

Glost   Or Glaze firing — that is to say the pots, usually biscuit fired, are glazed and then put in a second glaze or glost firing.

Green Ware   Dry unfired pots/clay.

Grog   Ground up and fired clay — it is added to clay bodies to reduce shrinkage and thermal shock.

Hard and Soft Ware   Meaning high and low fired pottery — degrees of heat.

Hollow Ware   Large, tall bellied shapes, rather than say dishes and plates.

Inlay   Meaning a type of decoration; hollows and pools are cut into the clay and topped up with clays and slips of another colour. Inlay is characteristically bold, hard edged and is usually worked on earthenware.

Iron Oxide   One of the most useful of all the oxides — is used in clay bodies, slips and glazes.

Kaolin   Meaning china clay.

Kidney   A rubber or metal kidney shaped tool — used for smoothing and scraping.

Kiln   The potter's fire, furnace or oven — can be fired by sea gas, bottled gas, coal, wood, oil or electricity.

Kneading   Meaning to work the wedged clay so that it is completely even in texture and free from air pockets.

Lawns   Meaning sieves, screens or gauzes, that are used to sieve slips and glazes.

Lead   Traditionally used in low temperature glazes — best used in its safe lead frit form.

Leather-Hard   Sometimes called soft green, cheese, or leather green, meaning clay that has started to dry but is still workable.

Lugs   Ear-shaped handles — can be made from cut discs of clay, usually found on the sides of kitchen crocks and garden pancheons.

Lustre   A decorative metalic coating.

Maquette   Meaning a working model or a prototype.

Marbled Ware   Pots decorated with coloured slips so as to look like marble — usually meaning brown and cream slipware dishes.

Master Mould   The main form from which all the others are made.

Needle   Called also a needle pricker — that is to say a spike set in a handle, used for cutting and spiking holes.

Overglaze   Painting — to paint glaze colours on a pot that has already been glazed and fired, and then to refire at a lower temperature — enamel.

Oxidation   In a gas, oil or wood fired kiln; meaning to have a clean firing with plenty of oxygen; oxides thus fired stay their oxide colour, for example green copper oxide stays green.

Placing   Meaning to carefully fill and pack a kiln.

Plaster of Paris   Potter's plaster, used to make moulds and the like.

Plastic   A good workable clay is described as — 'being plastic'.

Porcelain   A white translucent pottery.

Pug Mill   A machine used for clay mixing; waste clay goes in one end, and a 'sausage' of near workable clay is extruded out of the other.

Pyrometer   An instrument used to measure kiln temperature.

Raku Ware   Sometimes called 'Tea Ware', a low fired ware, made by the Japanese and used in their Tea Ceremony — now used to describe a course, well grogged clay body.

Reduction   To take away or reduce the oxygen during a firing — in a reduction firing, oxides give their metal colours, for example green copper oxides become red.

Rolling pin   A clay rolling tool, used to make slabs and sheets of clay.

Saddles   A type of kiln furniture — used when stacking plates and the like.

Saggars   Clay boxes, used in raw firings to protect pots from flames.

Salt Glaze   Used in open kilns, (wood etc) to form a characteristic thin, very attractive, glaze.

Sgraffito   Meaning to scratch — to cover a pot with a clay slip and then to scratch through and reveal the colour beneath.

Slips   Clay and water — used to decorate pots.

Smoking or Steaming   Used to describe the slow pre-heating during a biscuit firing — also sometimes used to describe a reduction firing.

Soaking   Meaning to keep the kiln contents at a steady heat.

Stoneware   Vitrified pottery — fired at over 1200°C.

Terra-Cotta   Unglazed brown earthenware.

Top-Loader   A kiln with a top lid.

Throwing   Meaning to make pots on a wheel.

Turning   To work a leather hard pot on the wheel with a turning tool.

Trailing   To decorate damp clay with squeezed trails of coloured slip.

Underglaze   Colours painted on unfired clay prior to subsequent glazing and firing.

Wire   A taut cheese wire used to cut clay.

Wax Resist   To paint pots with hot wax — the wax resists slips and glazes —used in decoration.

Wedging   To work clay so as to remove air pockets.

Whirler   Or Turn-table; sometimes also called a banding wheel — a metal stand that rotates and used when you want to decorate or work a slowly turning pot.

BIBLIOGRAPHY

THE DECORATED TILE
Austwick, J. B.   Published by Pitman, London 1980.

ANCIENT AMERICAN POTTERY
Bushnell, G. H. S. and Digby, A.   London 1955.

PIONEER POTTERY
Cardew, Michael   Published by Longman, London 1969.

POTTERY AND PORCELAIN
Hannover, E.   3 Vols, London 1925.

CERAMIC ART OF CHINA AND OTHER COUNTRIES OF THE FAR EAST
Honey, W. B.   London 1945.

V & A GUIDE TO THE COLLECTION OF TILES
Lane, A.   London 1960.

A POTTERS BOOK
Leach, Bernard   London 1940 and later edition

KENYAN AND HIS TRADITIONS
Leach, Bernard   Published by Faber and Faber, London 1966.

JAPANESE CERAMICS
Miller, R. A.   Tokyo and Rutland 1960.

CERAMICS FOR THE ARTIST POTTER
Norton, F. H.   Addison and Wesley, Cambridge, Mass 1956.

KILNS, DESIGN, CONSTRUCTION AND OPERATION
Rhodes, Daniel   Published by Chilton Co., Radnor Penn 1968.

KILNS AND KILN BUILDING
Searle, A. B.   Published by The Clayworker Press, London 1915.

TRIBAL CRAFTS OF UGANDA
Trowell, Margaret and Wachsmann, K. P.   London 1953.

INDEX

African pottery, 55–64
Art Deco designs, 109
Art Deco vase, 107–115
Arts and crafts, 34
Biscuit firing, 22, 31, 41, 72, 82, 93, 105, 114, 135
Box building, 78, 80
Building, 60
Bulls-eye slip design, 102
Burnishing, 17, 52, 53, 62

Calipers, 122
Casting, 14, 107–115, 123
Cast trimming, 114
Centering, 131
Chinese, 77
Chinese tray, 75–85
Claybench, 3
Clay drying, 53
Clay types, 5
Coiling, 11–12, 29, 36, 47–50, 58–61
Cottage jug, 127–137
Country workshop, 129

Decoration, 17, 30, 41, 57, 61, 63, 92
Design transferring, 79
Dolls, 118
Doll's head, 117–126
Domestic slipware, 87
Drying, 105, 135

Electric wheel, 130
Encaustic, 68
English medieval slipware, 65–74
English slipware, 85–96

Feathering, 100
Feet, 104
Fettling, 93, 114, 124, 126
Firing, 21, 23, 32, 42, 53, 62, 73, 82, 94, 105, 114, 126, 135
Forming, 38
French dolls, 119
French tile, 67
Fretting, 79

Glaze, 3, 19, 20, 31, 41
Glaze firing, 31, 42, 82, 94, 105, 114, 137
Glazing, 73, 82, 94, 105, 114
Gladstone pottery, 68
Glaze pouring, 115
Glaze sticks, 115

Gothic, 68
Grogged stoneware, 78
Grogging, 28, 59
Guide sticks, 71, 91

Haematite, 50
Handle pulling, 134, 136
Honey glaze, 87
Hump mould, 88, 103

Inlay, 17, 65–74
Incising, 18, 57, 63, 83

Jugs, 127–137
Jumeau doll, 119

Kidney tool, 62, 92
Kiln, 3, 21
Kiln furniture, 23
Kneading, 9, 27, 59

Lead glaze, 67
Lip pulling, 134, 135

Marbelling, 97–105
Minton and Co., 68
Modelling, 39, 40, 41, 49–50, 120–122
Mould, 58
Moulding, 13, 72, 102, 103
Mould keys, 122
Mould making, 69, 70, 90, 112, 123
Mould template, 89

Nazca pottery, 44
New England pottery, 97–105

Opening up, 132
Oxide, 50, 60

Pattern transferring, 69
Peruvian pottery, 44–54
Pie-crust rim, 98
Piercing, 75–85
Pinching, 11
Plaster, 13, 70, 111
Plaster box, 70, 90, 111, 123
Plaster casting, 111
Porcelain, 6, 117–126
Porcelain slip casting, 117–126
Portrait vase, 46
Press moulding, 90, 103
Pulling a handle, 136

Raku, 6, 26, 32
Recycling, 9–10
Red earthenware, 5
Rim, 59
Rim trimming, 104, 134
Rolling, 71, 91

Scraping, 61
Sgraffito, 19
Sieving, 20
Slabbing, 11–12, 75–85
Slab cutter, 78
Slab moulding, 65–74, 85–96, 97–105
Slab pressing, 92
Slip casting, 107–115, 117–126
Slip decoration, 135
Slip ground, 92, 101
Slip marbling, 97–105
Slip moulding, 122
Slips, 14, 18, 19, 50, 52, 72
Slip trailer, 94, 95
Slip trailing, 85–95
Slipware, 65–74, 85–95, 97–105
Slipware designs, 87
Soft soap, 123

Spouted pot, 43–56
Steaming and smoking, 105
Stoneware, 5
Stoneware firing, 82
Storage, 3

Throwing, 15, 16, 127–137
Throwing tools, 130, 131
Thumbpot, 11, 28, 37
Tile, 67
Tile pressing, 71
Toft, Thomas, 86, 87
Tools, 4

Underglaze, 19

Victorian doll's head, 117–126

Wax resist, 119
Wedging, 27, 59, 78
Wheel, 4, 15, 16, 127–137
White earthenware, 5
Wire cuter, 80
Working model, 110, 121
Workshop, 1–2, 129